The Religious Ideas of Harriet Beecher Stowe: Her Gospel of Womanhood

GAYLE KIMBALL

Studies in Women and Religion
Volume Eight

The Edwin Mellen Press
New York and Toronto

Library of Congress Cataloging in Publication Data

Kimball, Gayle
    The religious ideas of Harriet Beecher Stowe.

    (Studies in women and religion ; v. 8)
    Bibliography: p.
    1. Stowe, Harriet Beecher, 1811-1896--Religion and
ethics. 2. Stowe, Harriet Beecher, 1811-1896--Political
and social views. 3. Religion in literature.
4. Women in literature 5. Woman (Christian theology)
I. Title. II. Series.
PS2958.R4K55 1982   813'.3   82-20377
ISBN 0-88946-544-4

Studies in Women and Religion
ISBN 0-88946-549-5

            The Edwin Mellen Press
            P.O. Box 450
            Lewiston, New York   14092

Printed in the United States of America

FOR ELIZABETH CADY STANTON

who looked objectively at

religious teachings about women

ACKNOWLEDGEMENTS

My appreciation to Craig Stacey, Robert Michaelson,
Murray Markland and Elizabeth Clark for their editorial
contributions.

Gayle Kimball

California State University, Chico
Chico, California

September 1982

CONTENTS

LIST OF ABBREVIATIONS FOR HBS' NOVELS

Agnes =	*Agnes of Sorrento*, 1862
OTF =	*Oldtown Folks*, 1869
Pearl =	*The Pearl of Orr's Island*, 1862
PWT =	*Pink and White Tyranny*, 1871
PP =	*Poganuc People*, 1878
Neighbors =	*We and Our Neighbors*, 1875
UTC =	*Uncle Tom's Cabin*, 1852
Wife =	*My Wife and I*, 1871

INTRODUCTION

In the mid-nineteenth century a group of female religious activists challenged the traditional male domination of the American churches with their own powerful concept of what Harriet Beecher Stowe referred to as the "gospel of womanhood." Stowe was a major preacher of the redeeming power of women.[1] Her novels were best sellers, the bibles of the "Sentimental Love Religion" both in the United States and Great Britain.[2] After the publication of *Uncle Tom's Cabin*, for example, she received the warmest welcome given to any American by the British until Charles Lindberg made his pioneering airflight in the following century. The sheer volume in sales of her novels, both in America and abroad, merits the study of HBS as expressive of the popular thought of her era.

While HBS was one of the most prolific proponents of the idea of the angelic and civilizing impact of pious women, this view was widespread in Victorian society in both England and America. HBS did not originate the idea of the lady as savior; it was popularized in the eighteenth century with such novels as Samuel Richardson's *Clarissa*. It continued in the works of Victorian sentimental novelists, as well as in the sermons and writings of clergymen such as Horace Bushnell and Henry Ward Beecher.

HBS also helped transform the Protestant notion of the family. Luther and Calvin had replaced the priest with the male head of the household; Calvin taught that the father was the "representative of God and the Christian magistrate in the family." Essentially he was the head of his own little church, an idea elaborated upon by the Puritans who settled New England. Further, patriarchal Protestantism vigorously rejected Roman Catholic veneration of the Virgin Mary. But HBS popularized a new kind of Protestant Mariology:

the Virgin Mother was replaced by the self-sacrificing wife
and mother. HBS proclaimed the mother as the spiritual head
of the family, responsible for the religious education of
children, and the guardian of morality.

In her era, the Victorian age, women's and men's worlds
were divided: the inner domestic sphere was assigned to
women and the outer sphere to men. This division was agree-
able to men of the Jacksonian era and after, to those who
poured their energies into taming the frontier and reveling
in the power struggles of nineteenth century capitalism and
nationalism. Men made money while women prayed, providing
the work force and membership for the church missionary
outreach, although male clergy directed women's labor.
Harriet Beecher Stowe added her voice to those which advocated turning piety over to women and business and politics
to men.

HBS was the daughter and sister of two of the most
prominent preachers of their generations--Lyman Beecher and
Henry Ward Beecher. All of her brothers were ministers, as
was her husband Calvin and her son Charles. The Beecher
family was a significant force in the formulation of nineteenth century Protestant beliefs, and their own lives were
in turn powerfully influenced by those religious notions.
Encircled by discussion of theological issues her entire
life, HBS was well acquainted with the important issues of
Protestant thought.

To be a Beecher meant to be a preacher, yet that was a
career which custom did not accord to women. The highest
compliment which Lyman paid to his daughters was to tell
them they were like boys. What then was a nineteenth century woman to do who was imbued from the cradle with an
impelling sense of the duty of the soldiers of Christ to
combat Satan in the world? Only one of her sisters, Mary,
was content to follow the female norm by raising a family

without entering into public life. Another, Catharine, used
education as her pulpit to preach that women exemplified the
highest moral code of self-sacrificing service as mothers,
teachers and nurses. Their half-sister, Isabella, was an
advocate of the women's movement and the radical Woodhull
sisters. Writing was one of the few other channels of
expression open to middle class women; HBS chose the pen as
her crusading instrument and produced *Uncle Tom's Cabin*, the
most popular novel of her century, as an extended sermon
against slavery and for recognition of the redeeming powers
of women. (See the annotated bibliography for a description
of her novels.)

Stowe's thought is portrayed as seriously in her novels
as in her letters or non-fictional essays and books. The
heroines of her novels are vehicles for her point of view.
The most obvious example is Dolly, the main character of her
semi-autobiographical novel *Poganuc People* (1878). Dolly's
quest for a beautiful and accepting church mirrored Harriet's
search. HBS left no doubt as to which characters, like
Dolly, speak for her point of view and those obnoxious
characters who present the opposing opinion, such as meddling
Aunt Maria in *My Wife and I* (1871). HBS had children in
mind among the readers of her novels so it takes little sub-
tlety to determine the characters to be heeded and those to
be scorned.

No previous study has focused much attention on Stowe's
advocacy of women as the central agents of salvation, yet
that concept is the basic foundation of her work. She
rejected the New England theology conversion formula of her
childhood as propagated by overly speculative male clergy.
Literary romanticism provided a framework for her glorification of women who more often trusted their hearts than their
minds. She believed that one must give allegiance to some
denomination other than to the Unitarians. She turned to

the non-Calvinistic Episcopal Church because the romantic
sensuousness of its ritual and its acceptance of all sincere
believers without a specific salvation experience appealed
to her. She also maintained the reformist zeal of her
childhood religion and thereby became involved in the reform
movement she considered of primary import--the abolition of
slavery. She believed that slavery, especially since it was
destructive of family ties, deserved her first attention.
Her second allegiance was to the support of the rights of
women, a group oppressed in many ways similar to those in
acknowledged slavery.

     In her novels HBS portrayed women as the most effective
leaders of souls to Christ. She depicted the male clergy
mired in dry theological disputes and as ineffectual shep-
herds of needy spirits. The only study of Stowe which has
concentrated solely on her religious thought, Charles Foster's
The Rungless Ladder, missed this central point of her writings.
Foster contends that Stowe was "a more masculine than a
feminine artist." He gives as an example her *Oldtown Folks*
about which he concludes, "We are almost completely unconscious that the book is the work of a woman; we feel we are
being addressed by a thoroughly mature and full-blooded
Puritan-Yankee like Lyman Beecher."[3] Foster's thesis is
that Stowe, tormented by the death of two sons, who had not
undergone the requisite conversion experience, was driven by
anxiety. Her "inner compulsions" stemming from her Calvinist upbringing were resolved by her move to the Episcopal
Church. He concluded, however, that she gave her "final
yes" to Calvinism in her novel *The Minister's Wooing* when
she made her character Reverend Hopkins a prime example of
the theologian Jonathan Edwards' principle of "disinterested
benevolence." Hopkins unselfishly gave up his claim to his
fiancée when her previous lover, who had been believed
drowned on a sea voyage, unexpectedly returned. However,

Foster did not recognize the fact that Hopkins, for all his
principles and unselfishness, was painted by HBS as ludicrous and ineffective in saving souls. It was the heroine,
Mary Scudder, who exemplified Stowe's ideal of Christian
virtue and efficacy rather than the Calvinist Hopkins.

Stowe's books and letters are replete with key words
and phrases which repetitively project her feminine symbols
and myths. Her types include: women saviors, either young
and virginal or motherly; ineffectual male clergy tangled up
in the inconsistencies of their theological systems; and
well-meaning sons and husbands dependent on mothers and
wives for spiritual inspiration and insight as her father
Lyman depended on his wife Roxana and her husband Calvin
depended on Harriet. In her thirty-odd works, and numerous
articles and letters, HBS provided her readers with example
after example of the redeeming power of women. Hers is a
case study of the cult of womanhood. She was a tireless
preacher, exhorting womankind to its appointed role as
"mediators of salvation endowed with privileged communi-
cation with the other world."[4]

The legacy of her thought continued into the twentieth
century. Her grand-niece Charlotte Perkins Gilman, a major
feminist writer of the first quarter of the century, continued Stowe's theme that women are skilled in motherly love,
practical service and affirmation of the good, while men get
caught in abstract speculation about the after-life and
stress the vengeful judgment of an angry God. Feminist
theologians such as Mary Daly and Rosemary Ruether have
dropped the emphasis on motherly love, but continue to
search for female symbols.

Even though Stowe's novels now rest in the children's
section of the library, like other American classics which
avoid realistic male-female relationships, the struggle
against male domination of church policy, leadership, and

imagery is still a vital issue in modern theology while the
search for an identity for women in religion is still ardently
pursued.

NOTES

[1]Hereafter abbreviated as HBS (a precedent established
by Theosophists who refer to their founder, Helena P. Blavatsky
as HPB). See Appendix 1 for a chronology of Stowe's life.
The roots of belief in women's spiritual power are deep,
going back to ancient history and the mother goddesses, to
Biblical references, as in Revelation, to the woman "clothed
with the sun, and the moon under her feet" who brought forth
a son to rule the nation (Revelation: 12:1-2). In England,
before Richardson, Spencer's *Faerie Queene* (1590s) includes
heroines who are spiritual leaders. Una, for example,
encourages the Redcrosse Knight to fight the Dragon of
Error. Britomart, a female warrior, saves Amoret from a
wicked magic spell. Examples of other redemptive women
include Boethius' Lady Philosophy, St. Francis' Lady Poverty,
Dante's Beatrice, and Petrarch's Laura.

[2]See Leslie Fiedler, *Love and Death in the American
Novel*, (New York: Criterion Books, 1970).

[3]Charles Foster, *The Rungless Ladder*, p. 202.

[4]Françoise Basch, *Relative Creatures: Victorian Women
in Society and the Novel*, (New York: Schocken, 1970), p. 71.

CHAPTER ONE

SALVATION SOUGHT

LITCHFIELD

In 1810 Lyman and Roxana Beecher moved to Litchfield, Connecticut, where Lyman became pastor of the Congregational Church. A year later Roxana gave birth to Harriet, her seventh child.[1] In time the household grew to include two Negro bond servants, an orphaned cousin, the two children born after Harriet, and Roxana's sister Mary, who was a frequent visitor. There were often other guests including many clergymen.

The Beechers' was a lively home. Lyman's eldest and favorite daughter Catharine described his daily recreations as "frolics" with his children. His second wife, Harriet Porter, whom he married a year after Roxana's death in 1816, reported that the Beecher house was full of great cheerfulness and comfort. She was pleased by her introduction to "the best of people." Stimulation was also provided by the visits of young students from Judge Tapping Reeve's law school and the Litchfield Female Academy which Harriet began to attend at age eight.

With her father preparing the way for the millenium, and the Litchfield house overflowing with ten children, pets, and visitors, young Harriet found her private world in books. She began reading at age five, fascinated by Cotton Mather's *Magnalia*, and by Scott and Byron. She memorized Biblical passages and hymns at an early age.

Her memories of childhood were bitter-sweet, with so many other children, her mother's early death, and her father's preoccupation with his ministry. She felt that the Beecher children were raised by an "uncaressing let-alone system."[2] They were washed, dressed, sent to school and

then to bed as early as possible, with no special children's
toys, books or holidays, except for Thanksgiving. HBS
represented her father as too concerned with demonstrating
the "consistency of decrees and accountability" to take the
time to find out what his young children were thinking.[3]
However, he loved them dearly, writing to Roxana that he
could not think of her or the babies without tears. Harriet
was left with "a sense of personal insignificance as a
child, weaned upon the absolute need for passive obedience
to adults."[4]

The desire to please Lyman by producing a genuine
salvation experience which fulfilled his spiritual requirements was magnified by emotional needs. Nevertheless,
Catharine, who assumed leadership when her mother died, had
the strength to rebel against his requirements for salvation.
Harriet, tormenting herself throughout her teenage years,
finally followed Catharine's rejection of Lyman's theology.[5]
Lyman advised Catharine, as a lost sinner, to cry for mercy,
"remembering that it is your duty to do that which you cry
to God to help you to do."[6] But Catharine did not believe
that she had the ability to satisfy Lyman and his God.
Neither had she a sense of her own wickedness, feeling that
if she were born without the willingness to be saved it was
not her fault, in much the same way that a man born with a
weakness for alcohol was to be pitied rather than blamed.
Nor did she believe she should feel guilty when in fact she
made every effort to do good.

The occasion for Catharine's rebellion was not so much
her own inability to produce the necessary conviction of
sin--never having any fear of punishment or hope of rewards,
she said--as the death at sea of her fiancé, Alexander
Fisher. He was a Yale professor who drowned in 1822. He
had not had the experience of saving grace, but she could
not accept the orthodox view that such a fine human being

would burn in hell. She revolted against the theology of
original sin altogether, stating that the notion of natural
depravity was a fiction invented by Augustine, and that the
Calvinist notion of Free Agency was actually fatalism thinly
disguised. Sin resulted not from a depraved nature but
depraved action. An educational evangelist, she placed her
faith in the ability of a Christian home and school to shape
a child's moral development in a positive way.

Instead of theology, Catharine relied on her own reason
and common sense which permitted her to "deduce from the
works of God a system of natural religion far superior to
that of theologians." She explained, "I have a better
chance than any learned men, any metaphysicians, any theologians, to come to correct conclusions" because she was not
biased by membership in any theological school or party.[7]
Her common sense told her that God does not require anything
of humans that we are not capable of performing. She explained,
"God saved those who seemed to want to be saved, not merely
those who had passed through a conversion experience."[8] Nor
is his creation anything but good: the infant, she said, is
the creation of God, "and we impeach his wisdom or goodness
when we deny that it is rightly constructed."[9] Heaven is
attainable for all those who devoutedly try to love God and
wish to do his will. HBS' views of God were also shaped by
her brother Edward's gentle notion of God; and gradually she
exchanged the stern majestic deity of her childhood for
their more loving God.

The glorification of the spiritual power of women, a
hallmark of HBS' philosophy, was also derived from her
sister. While Lyman had always insisted on the pre-eminent
function of the male clergy in leading the populace out of
the pits of damnation, Catharine maintained that this responsibility fell to women, especially in their roles as educators
and homemakers. She felt that when women are properly

educated, "the salt is scattered throughout the land to
purify and save."[10]

Catharine's belief in a loving God who rewarded all who
attempted to please Him was a harkening back to her mother's
persuasions. Raised an Episcopalian, Roxana became a Calvinist upon her marriage to Lyman, and accepted the idea of
man's depraved inability to do right. But Roxana never gave
up the idea that God was a merciful guide, giving wounds
only in order to heal. She rejected the doctrine of Bellamy
and Hopkins that virtue consists in taking delight in God's
glory even if it requires one's own or others' damnation.
She stated that "God will not illumine heaven in his glory...
by sacrificing helpless, unoffending creatures to eternal
torment."[11] In her daily conduct and character and in her
faith and unassuming kindness and patience, Lyman found
Roxana the best and only example of that disinterested
benevolence which was the highest virtue in the New Haven
theology.

After Roxana's death Catharine served as Harriet's
surrogate mother, most noticeably when Harriet went to live
with her in Hartford at age thirteen. Before then Catharine
guided her by letter, asking her to "learn to stand and sit
straight, and hear what people say to you, and sit still in
your class, and learn to sew and knit well."[12] Harriet was
profoundly influenced by Catharine's religious ideas adopting
the belief that "sin alone is evil and from that Christ will
keep us."[13] In her novel The Minister's Wooing (1859) she
reflected Catharine's struggle over Fisher's fate. The
intellectual Mrs. Marvyn is disconsolate when her sailor son
James is lost at sea, without church membership. Esther in
HBS' novel Old Town Folks is a combination of Harriet and
Catharine, another thoughtful woman who is unable to experience the turbulent emotional conviction of her own sinfulness.
In the same novel Emily Rossiter is driven from orthodoxy by

the harsh Dr. Stern, representing Nathaniel Emmons, whose
sermons burdened Catharine while she was visiting Fisher's
parents after his death. Emmons made her feel, Catharine
explained, that humans were "mere machines, and all our
wickedness was put into us; and then we were required to be
willing to be forever miserable."[14]

Although she adopted much of Catharine's religious
bent, Harriet resented her authority. In Hartford HBS was
in the middle of composing her epic poem *Cleon* when Catharine
"pounced" upon her and set her to studying Butler's *Analogy*
instead.[15] In her novels there are frequently a pair of
sisters, the older one dominating the meek younger sister,
as in *Pearl of Orr's Island* where Miss Roxy puts her "sharp
heavy stamp" on every opinion of her poetic younger sister,
Miss Ruey.

HARTFORD

In 1824 Harriet was sent to help Catharine with her
Hartford school for girls. After the death of her fiancé,
Catharine had turned to one of the few occupations open to
women at the time: she established the Hartford Female
Seminary in that growing town of 5,000. At Catharine's
school Harriet studied Latin, French, Italian, painting and
drawing, in addition to other standard courses. In 1829 she
became a full-time instructor, teaching Latin, rhetoric and
composition. Her major focus was not on her studies, however.
She was most occupied with her religious struggles, her
sins, and groping with the definition of God's nature.

Her quest for salvation came to an early climax at age
fourteen when, on a visit from Hartford to her father's
Litchfield church, she thought that she had experienced
conversion. Lyman preached a communion service where he
spoke in the name of Christ, "Behold, I call you no longer
servants, but friends." A friend was what HBS wanted, as

she was without her mother, a middle child lost among
Catharine's Hartford pupils. She told her father that she
had come to Christ; he hugged her, wept, and announced that
a new flower had bloomed in heaven that day. She participated
in her first communion service on November 1, 1825. But her
conversion remained incomplete: she had no conviction of
her sins. She resolved to cope with this dilemma by trusting
in Christ to give it to her.

The major difficulty of Harriet's life was this struggle
to be saved. She was pious and conscientious to an extreme,
but could not match the salvation formula of New England
theology and its requisite conviction of sin and depravity
as deserving eternal punishment. Later in her life she
advised her minister son Charles to "step out of formulas,"
although not to specifically preach against them.[16] However,
the book that she said influenced her second to the Bible,
Richard Baxter's *Saint's Everlasting Rest*, taught "how vile
sin is, and that by the covenant thou has transgressed, the
least sin deserves eternal death."[17] She was also influenced by Jonathan Edwards who carefully studied the conversion
experience, defining its marks and signs for New England
theology. He described its initial anguish and fear over
sin and the depraved state of one's soul to the final calm-
ness and delight in the beauty of God's creation.

When she returned to Hartford, after hearing her father's
sermon, her pastor applied the standard formula to her
experience, and was not so accepting as Lyman had been. He
quizzed her as to whether she would be happy to be alone
with God in the universe and was she cognizant of the deceit-
fulness of her heart. These sorts of questions threw her
into a turmoil which lasted into her twenties, sapping her
energies and confidence. Her struggle troubled her mentors
Catharine, her brother Edward (a minister at Boston's Park
Street Church) and Lyman. She believed that the Bible made

no allowance for sin, but reasoned that she was to be pitied
instead of blamed for her inability not to sin, for her
pride and selfish desire to be loved. If it were ordained
that she was to sin, if she could not avoid sin, why should
she be punished for her fate and her inability? She could
not resolve this issue of sin, later deciding to trust in
the Biblical promise that clarity would be given in the
future life.

She also pondered the nature of God, torn between the
Calvinist God of revival preaching and the more gentle God
of Catharine and Edward. The former was a majestic King of
Kings, so remote that, "everything but the most distant
reverential affection seems almost sacrilegious."[18] The
latter was kindly and benign, a view she later accepted in
her understanding of the person of Jesus. She feared that
to view God as a caring being would detract from his majesty
and her reverence. She concluded that Baxter's description
of God was her own: "Thou shalt be his child, and he thy
Father, externally embraced in the arms of that love."[19] At
age eighteen she returned to where she had begun, to trust
in Christ as her best friend. She explained that, "Christians
in general do not seem to look to Him as their best friend,
or realize anything of his unalterable love. They speak
with a cold, vague, reverential awe, but do not speak as if
in the habit of close and near communion."[20] She decided,
with the counsel of her Uncle Foote, to count just the
golden hours, and resolved to cease brooding and to start
reaching out to other people.[21]

CINCINNATI

In Cincinnati Catharine founded the Western Female
Institute, and again Harriet's energies were consumed by
teaching and by her continuing depressing concern for her
sins. She explained that "Thought, intense emotional thought,

has been my disease."[22]   She did muster the concentration to
write a children's geography book.   She had no great love of
the city where she was to spend eighteen years and never
used it as a setting for her fiction.

At twenty-four, Harriet was finally released from her
teaching burdens to assume those of another kind when she
married her father's associate at Lane, widower Calvin
Stowe.   He was nine years older than she, a graduate of
Bowdoin and Andover Theological Seminary, and a Hebrew
scholar.   Often melancholy, he was plagued by what she named
the "hypos."   He was stocky and balding.   The same year that
they were married she gave birth to twin daughters, the
first of seven children.   These were difficult years for the
Stowes, for often Lane was unable to pay its professors more
than half of their promised salary.   Harriet took in boarders
and wrote short stories and articles for magazines to augment
Calvin's salary.   He encouraged her in her writing, believing
that it was God's will, "written in the book of fate."

A collection of her short stories was published by
Harper and Brothers in 1843.   *The Mayflower* contains rudi-
ments of themes developed later: the angelic uplifting
qualities of women such as "Aunt Mary" or the wife as a
"guardian in virtue"; the uplifting impact of beauty; the
importance of capacity for feeling rather than intellect;
and the importance of suffering in turning one toward God.
As compared with later works, the difference found in Stowe's
early stories is that women as saviors are not yet developed
or dominant.   Women are devoted wives or magical, pretty
fairies who twinkle about, but they don't have the power to
transform lives in the same way as they do in later novels.
Men do the saving, as does the dying pure young minister in
"Uncle Lot", or the male friend responsible for saving the
drunkard whose wife cannot save him in "Let Every Man Mind
His Own Business."

HBS was often in poor health, especially after her
pregnancies, when her vision was impaired for months. After
her fifth pregnancy she escaped to a water-cure in Vermont
for almost a year, only to return to active children, temperamental servants, and a husband with "the blues." She felt
herself to be a household drudge. She did not feel sure yet
of her salvation, writing to her husband that her pride was
not yet subdued, her heart not wholly renewed, "Christ not
fully formed in me," for she had not prayed enough, nor had
she or Calvin "yet taken the almighty hand that is held out
to us...." She resolved in 1842 to prepare to die and to
live for God.[23]

The suicide of her brother George in 1843 shook her
soul "like an earthquake." She did not feel at peace for
two years afterward, stung with worry over her future life
and her continuing "sin" of concern for what people thought
of her. She wished fervently that Christ would "make his
abode" within her soul and Calvin's, since life was a "dreary,
black monotonous vacancy."[24] She hoped that when one prayed
for, worked for, and believed in conversion, results would
follow. In her search for conversion she had glimpses of
"the most sweet and heavenly communion with Christ," and
visions of him in a regal palace in a secret room where he
sat alone, "a god-like immortal youth dispensing outpourings
of love." She believed that "Christ is all" and an ever
present help, although not satisfied with her fleeting
glimpses of him.[25]

In 1845 her despair again lifted--all changed, she
reported. She resolved again to trust Christ, like Peter
and James who let down their nets at his command, without
questioning his reasoning.[26] She had strength enough to
accept the death from cholera of her infant son Charles in
1847, having no doubts about his salvation "among the
blessed."[27] She had also achieved a new confidence in her

own spiritual life, for although she considered herself
"poor trash", she asserted: "I am his chosen one for all
that, and I shall reign with him," whom she described as her
betrothed.[28]

BRUNSWICK

Both Harriet and Calvin were relieved when in 1850 he
was offered a teaching position at Bowdoin College in Brunswick, Maine. HBS loved the Maine seacoast, its "picturesque"
fiords and lakes, the "white winged" ships from India or
China, the pine forest and sandy plains.

Calvin's salary remained meager, around three hundred
dollars less than their expenses. Consequently, Harriet,
with aid from Catharine, organized a school where she taught
for an hour a day in addition to doing her own mending,
shopping, cooking, nurturing her seventh child, plus writing
Uncle Tom's Cabin. A loving mother, she somehow found time
to read to her children for two hours every evening, especially from Scott's novels. She felt buoyed by her love of
Christ. The former void in her heart filled with a sense of
security and peace because of "what He gave me years ago
when He wrote His name in my heart." Whenever she called,
He responded, "I am here," so "now all is joy," she stated.[29]

She became involved in the slavery issue, aroused by
the enforcement of the Fugitive Slave Law of 1850. Her
family encouraged her to write something to help arouse the
country to the plight of the slaves. She began a series of
books about slavery: Uncle Tom's Cabin (the first chapter
was completed in April of 1851); The Key to Uncle Tom's
Cabin (1853), to provide documentation in support of her
first novel; Dred (1856) to probe possible solutions for the
slavery question since the South was not providing any
answers; and Men of Our Times (1868), mainly about Civil War
political and military leaders.

It has been suggested by various biographers that HBS
had personal motivations in her response to slavery. Stowe
herself explained that "much that is in that book...had its
root in the awful scenes and bitter sorrows of that summer"
when her infant son died in the cholera epidemic of 1847.[30]
She learned, she said, what a slave mother felt when her
child was taken from her. She also identified herself with
black women because of her domestic duties, her never ending
labors to take care of her children on a meager income and
with a melancholy husband. She described her situation in
Cincinnati to Calvin as "excessively harassing and painful."
She determined "not to be a mere domestic slave, without
even the leisure to excel in my duties...."[31] She and
Calvin were also in temperamental opposition; he wishing for
an orderly, systematic household, she scattering the newspaper about and wishing to spend more time in the garden
than in the kitchen; he complaining about his low spirits,
she urging him to put less emphasis on his studies and
church organizations and more reliance on Christ. The
slavery novels expressed her frustration with her domestic
scene, that is, her identification of her unpaid domestic
drudgery with the work performed by slaves, as well as her
judgment as to the evils of dislocation of family life of
slaves and their owners.

The slavery novels are also transitional in her development of women as saviors. Uncle Tom is portrayed as motherly,
submissive, feminine; little Eva's death saves onlookers
moved by her angelic innocence; Rachel, the Quaker mother,
is a model of piety, but a mature woman is not yet central.
Dred was originally titled Nina Gordon but Stowe killed Nina
off after the historical attack on Sumner in the Senate and
focused instead on her character Dred, the black prophet
hidden in the swamps. The slave woman Milly is more loving
and Christian than he, but the focus is not on her.

ANDOVER

In 1852 Calvin accepted a better paying position teaching in Andover, Massachusetts, where they lived until 1864.
HBS received visits from abolitionists such as Sojourner
Truth and Frederick Douglas. She wrote *Dred*, visited President Lincoln, collected petitions against slavery, and wrote
a column for *The Independent*.

There Harriet tried to give her children rest from the
religious torment she had suffered. She attempted to act as
a mediator, for example, advising her twins that a mother's
love is God revealed; "love me, then God asks no more--he
sends me to you as his representative...."[32] She taught her
children that no souls are lost except those who willfully
resist God's love. They should pray, read the Bible, and
wait for God who "pursues every soul...till every possible
means of restoration has been tried."[33]

In Andover religious doubts surfaced again when her
favorite son Henry, a Dartmouth student, was drowned while
swimming in the Connecticut River in 1857. Henry, like
Alexander Fisher three decades earlier, sought to live as a
Christian ought to, though in a letter to his mother he said
he might not be what the world called a Christian, not
having had the conviction of sin and the sense of a new
nature. After his death her earlier fears spoke again:

> You trusted in God, did you? You believed
> that He loved you? You had perfect confidence
> that He would never take your child till the work
> of grace was mature! Now He has hurried him into
> eternity without a moment's warning, without
> preparation, and where is he now?

These were precisely the same concerns of her girlhood. She
dismissed them this time as irrational, an attack of the
Devil trying to separate her from Christ, and dishonorable
to a loving God. She trusted that Jesus had "taken my dear
one to his bosom." After her renewal of her Christ-centered

faith, her dismissal of the need for the salvation signs
required by evangelicals and the stern Calvinist God, she
asserted that "the Enemy has left me in peace." Thus she
seemed to equate Calvinist teachings of the need for a
salvation experience with the torment of the Devil, as it
would be erroneous to "assume that a thing which would be in
its very nature, unkind, ungenerous, and unfair as to send
an innocent child to hell would be done by God." She reasoned that she could not be more capable of love and dis-
interestedness than God: "He invented mothers' hearts, and
He certainly has the pattern in His own."[34]

However, the issue of salvation was not yet put to
rest. She wrote *The Minister's Wooing*, published in 1859,
to resolve some of the questions reawakened by Henry's
death. The novel returned to the New England setting which
she had used in her collection of short stories published as
The Mayflower.

HBS rejected the severity of the salvation formula
which required everyone to reach to top rung of disinterested
benevolence. One of her spokespersons is a black woman,
Candace, *(MW)* who states that "generate or unregenerate,
d'all one to me." Candace's view of a Christian is a person
who lovingly acts to help others, especially the poor.
Candace also points out that "I'm clr dar' considerable more
o' de 'lect dan people tink," since Jesus died for our
sins.[35] Candace had a simple faith and did not torment
herself with doctrinal issues of salvation. She put emphasis
on deed not creed, for as Harriet believed, a good Christian
manifested salvation through kindness to others.

Agnes of Sorrento, although about Catholics in sixteenth
century Italy, also paints the central male religious figure
as extreme and cold in his theology; the heroine's love
saves the young hero rather than the priest. Agnes wonders
how the saints can be happy when some humans are damned,

reiterating the love of Christ for all and the cruelty of
saving only a few elect. In *The Pearl of Orr's Island*, the
major characters are also saved by the unselfish love and
example of the heroine, Mara. Thus, Stowe resolved the
fears created by her son's death by concluding that salvation was given to all those who sincerely open their hearts.

HARTFORD

In 1864 the Stowes moved to Hartford. After the Emancipation Proclamation was issued, she directed her energies
toward beautifying the mansion she had constructed in Hartford in 1863, giving up the active role she had played in
the abolitionist movement. *Dred*, published in 1856, was her
last anti-slavery book.

She turned her attention away from slavery to the evils
of city life, writing three books about New York society:
Pink and White Tyranny, 1871; *My Wife and I*, 1871; *We and
Our Neighbors*, 1875; and three others in contrast about New
England's past rural tranquility: *Old Town Folks*, 1870; *Old
Town Fireside Stories*, 1871; *Poganuc People*, 1878.

Her books written in Hartford reflect her rejection of
the ladder with one rung. In 1864 she turned to the Episcopal Church for its acceptance of all believers. Her attendance at the Episcopal service was encouraged by the marriage
of her daughter Georgianna to an Episcopal priest, by the
church membership of the twins, and by Calvin's retirement
from teaching religion. In all of her six post-war books,
the major characters are or become members of the Episcopal
church.

A character who resembled Harriet and Catharine is
Esther Avery in *Old Town Folks*. Like Mrs. Marvyn *(MW)*,
Esther is bright and pious but deeply troubled because she
has not had the requisite experience of saving grace.
Esther finds peace through accepting her husband Harry's

love, and in addition adopting his allegiance to the Episcopal Church and his non-theological simple certainties about
Christ's love. Harry explained, "we must trust the intuition
of our hearts above reason. That is what I am trying to
persuade Esther to do."[36] Miss Mehitable also is tortured
by her search for "that conversion which our father taught
us to expect as alchemists seek the philosopher's stone.
What have I not read and suffered at the hands of the theologians. We in ourselves are so utterly helpless--life is so
hard, so inexplicable, that we stand in perishing need of
some helping hand...." She rejected the thrust of theology
that "this unknown gift [of conversion] which no child of
Adam ever did compass of himself, is so completely in my own
power, that I am every minute of my life to be blamed for
not possessing it."[37]

Dolly, Harriet's semi-autobiographical self in *Poganuc
People*, also is drawn to the Episcopal Church by the beauty
of its services and by the Anglican Englishman that she
marries. St. James, in *We and Our Neighbors*, is yet another
example of a person wounded by New England severity who
finds so much solace in the Episcopal Church that he became
a priest.

HBS did not in any way modify her constant search to
save the souls of her major characters and of real people.
Revivals of the camp meeting variety were never very appealing to her as shown by her description of them in *Dred*
as in tune with "the primitive habits" of the participants,[38]
but she shared the evangelical quest to save souls. She
noted in *We and Our Neighbors* that the preaching of the
gospel "does produce in some cases the phenomenon called
conversion...."[39] Her solution to the problem of salvation
was the sacrament of love, as taught by Christ, and as best
illustrated on earth by self-sacrificing women. She expanded
upon the idea described earlier in *The Minister's Wooing*

of the home as a cloister and shrine, giving specific direc-
tions about how to beautify it and uplift neighbors and a cir-
cle of friends in *House and Home Papers, My Wife and I,* and
We and Our Neighbors. There is more attention given to home
life after the Civil War issues were settled, after her dismissal of the effectiveness of clergy as soul savers in *The Minister's Wooing,* and her turn to the accepting Episcopal Church.

Her last book, *Poganuc People,* was published in 1878.
After 1884 Calvin's health was too poor to make the voyage
to Florida, so HBS spent the rest of her life in Hartford.
She suggested to Calvin that he "put the affairs all into my
hands and let me manage them my own way."[40] She in turn was
cared for by the twins when her mind failed around 1890
until her death in 1896. Her belief in the necessity of a
"simple childlike faith" in Christ as love continued. The
last words she spoke were "I love you."

The major theme of Stowe's life is her search for
salvation, for herself and for her family. Had she been
able to match the formula with its requisite conviction of
her willful sinfulness causing just punishment in hell we
would not have the record of the impact of New England
theology described in her novels. If Calvin had made an
ample salary we would not have had the passionate identity
with slave women which produced the books that helped mobilize northern opinion against the institution of slavery.
She analyzed New England theology carefully, praising it for
the habits of serious introspection and inquiry it taught
the common people, blaming Jonathan Edwards for making
salvation only for those, like himself, who were spiritual
virtuosos. She turned to the Episcopal Church and yet
continued in her latter novels to examine New England theory,
so we have a fascinating record of the struggle of those in
her generation to confront Edwards and his heirs with a
changing society no longer rural and pastoral, no longer
giving indications of a coming millennium.

Notes

[1]Harriet was followed by Henry in 1813 and Charles in
1816.

[2]Harriet Beecher Stowe, *Men of Our Time*, (Hartford:
Hartford Publishers Co., 1868), p. 508.

[3]Ibid., p. 510.

[4]HBS, *Men of Our Time*, p. 506.

[5]Many scholars (Rourke, Johnston, Adams, May, Page
Smith) have affirmed that HBS' career was sparked by rebellion against the tenets of her father and husband. Rourke
sees her as revolting against "those absorbed, impervious,
masculine minds" which gave her so little recognition
(Rourke, *Trumpets of Jubilee*, p. 97). Her efforts to free
slaves were akin to her efforts to free herself from male
domination. Rourke identifies Hopkins *(MW)* and the ingenu-
ous Presbyterian minister "who sat quietly behind his face"
(Dred) shielding his real beliefs, as representatives of
Lyman whom HBS struck down in her novels. Adams too sees
HBS as oppressed by subservience to her father and his
religion of law (Adams, *Harriet Beecher Stowe*, p. 19). He
believed that she escaped to non-Calvinist Florida to pro-
mulgate her own religion of love.

[6]Barbara Cross, ed., *Autobiography of Lyman Beecher*,
(Cambridge, Mass.: Belknap Press, of Harvard Univ. Press,
first published in 1864, 1961), V. 1, p. 363.

[7]Mae Harveson, *Catharine Beecher: Pioneer Educator*,
(Phil: The Science Press Printing Co., 1932), pp. 160, 164.

[8]Catharine Beecher, *Commonsense Applied to Religions*,
(New York: Harper & Brothers, 1857). Quoted in Kathryn
Sklar, *Catharine Beecher: A Study in American Domesticity*,
(New Haven: Yale Univ. Press, 1973), p. 239.

[9]Harveson, *Catharine Beecher*, p. 99.

[10]Ibid., p. 181.

[11]Cross, ed., *Autobiography of Lyman Beecher*, V. 1, p. 117.

[12]Cross, ed., *Autobiography of Lyman Beecher*, V. 1, p. 352, 25 February 1822.

[13]Charles Stowe, *Harriet Beecher Stowe: The Story of Her Life*, (Boston and New York: Houghton Mifflin Co., 1911), p. 87.

[14]Cross, ed., *The Autobiography of Lyman Beecher*, V. 1, p. 366.

[15]Butler was an Anglican (d. 1752). He taught the moral government of God who rewards and punishes in this life and the next, and that "the present world is peculiarly fit to be a State of discipline for our improvement in virtue and piety." Joseph Butler, *The Analogy of Religion*, (New York: Frederick Ungar, 1961), p. 80.

[16]HBS to Charles, Mandrin, Florida, 7 March 1879, Folder 196, Schlesinger Archives.

[17]Richard Baxter, *The Saints' Everlasting Rest*, (London: Thomas Kelly, 1836), p. 53 (English Puritan, written in the 1650's).

[18]Charles Stowe, *Harriet Beecher Stowe*, p. 40, HBS to her family, 27 May 1828.

[19]Baxter, *The Saints' Everlasting Rest*, p. 14.

[20]Charles Stowe, *Harriet Beecher Stowe*, p. 48, July, 1829.

[21]Charles Stowe and Lyman Stowe, *Harriet Beecher Stowe: The Story of Her Life*, (Boston: Houghton Mifflin Co., 1911), p. 63. Also, Wilson, *Patriotic Gore*, p. 89.

[22]Charles Stowe, *Harriet Beecher Stowe*, p. 65, May 1833, letter to Georgianna May.

[23]HBS to Calvin, Buffalo, New York, 4 September 1842, Folder 67, Schlesinger Archives.

[24]HBS to Calvin, 31 August--3 September 1844, Folder 70, Schlesinger Archives.

[25]HBS to Calvin, Walnut Hills, 24 September 1844,
Folder 70, Schlesinger Archives.

[26]Cross, ed., *Autobiography of Lyman Beecher*, V. 2,
p. 371. Letter written 21 June 1845.

[27]Taylor and Beecher had not preached infant damnation
since no moral decisions could be made by a baby.

[28]Fields, *Life and Letters of Harriet Beecher Stowe*,
p. 169, letter to Calvin from Andover, around 1852.

[29]HBS to Calvin, 1851, Folder 75, Schlesinger Archives.

[30]Charles Stowe, *Harriet Beecher Stowe*, p. 199, 16
February 1853, to Englishwoman Mrs. Follen.

[31]Wilson, *Crusader in Crinoline*, p. 204.

[32]HBS to the twins, Andover, 6 May 1859, Folder 103,
Schlesinger Archives.

[33]HBS to the twins, 5 or 31 May 1859, Folder 103,
Schlesinger Archives.

[34]Charles Stowe, *Harriet Beecher Stowe*, pp. 321, 322
for the above quotations.

[35]HBS, *The Minister's Wooing*, pp. 280, 348.

[36]HBS, *Old Town Folks*, V. 2 (New York: AMS Press,
1967, V. 9-10, first published in 1869), p. 57, p. 81.

[37]Ibid., V. 1, p. 248.

[38]HBS, *Dred*, V. L. (New York: AMS Press, 1967, V. 3
and 4, first published in 1869), p. 306.

[39]HBS, *We and Our Neighbors*, (New York: AMS Press,
1967, V. 13, first published in 1875), p. 413.

[40]HBS to Calvin, 3 September 1884, Folder 70, p. 3
Schlesinger Archives.

CHAPTER TWO
A Rejection of the New England Theology Salvation Formula

THE PURITAN FORMULA

HBS' theological cradle was the Calvinistic New England Puritanism taught by Jonathan Edwards, and modified by his pupils Joseph Bellamy and Samuel Hopkins. Yale President Timothy Dwight and his pupils Nathaniel Taylor and Lyman Beecher in turn qualified Hopkins' systematic theology in an attempt to accommodate real freedom of the will. Though HBS rejected much of New England theology, she continued to manifest an ambivalent attitude toward it. Her thought was shaped by reaction to New England theology.

Calvinism offered a clear statement of the human condition--depraved on account of the Original Sin, humans are deserving of hell fire unless they experience a preordained conversion and receive irresistible saving grace. The conversion experience is central, for "a natural man hath no God in any thing," explained the Puritan Thomas Hooker (d. 1647).[1] The first step in the conversion formula is conviction of one's sin and the realization that one is not a true Christian. Man can do no good work to earn his salvation. As HBS could not achieve the first requisite of the salvation formula, this was a major reason for her defection from Calvinism. She concluded that Calvinism could be "grim" and "ferocious".[2]

Some found it hard to exist with the potency stripped from their acts; thus early in the seventeenth century Arminianism surfaced, advocating a human's ability to work toward salvation.[3] Although considered a major heresy, Arminianism was kindred to Puritan Covenant Theology shaped in the Westminister Confession, 1643, and formally adopted

in New England in the Cambridge Platform of 1648. Federal
or Covenant theology permitted Calvinists to be more active:
God agreed to limit his power for his chosen people so that
if one availed oneself of the means of salvation, one could
reasonably expect to be saved through the fulfillment of the
compact; the sign of the new covenant was not male circumci-
sion but baptism. Preachers such as Thomas Hooker taught
that if the sinner obeyed God's will and prepared for salvation with righteous actions and a humble heart, God would
likely grant it. HBS gave an example of this "activist"
view in her novel *Old Town Folks* (1869). Her character
Horace Holyoke's Calvinist grandmother reads Bellamy daily
and accepts his belief that the sinner can not will to do
good--yet she believed that by exhortation she could direct
people's wills toward salvation.[4]

This controversy over the sinner's ability to prepare
for salvation arose early in the New England experience.
Anne Hutchinson was banished in 1638 because she had condemned ministers for teaching a covenant of works, rather
than grace. She lectured to her weekly gatherings that the
sinner must "stand still and wait for Christ to do all for
him."[5] Although she was a follower of John Cotton, hers was
a minority voice: she was condemned as an antinomian and
exiled from the Bay Colony.

The movement toward belief in the efficacy of free will
and actions culminated in the preachings of Cotton Mather:
"Try whether you can't give that consent; if you can, 'tis
done."[6] HBS saw the teaching of free agency as arising out
of social and governmental changes, namely government by the
people, explaining that "new forms of doctrinal statement...
grow out of new forms of society."[7] Calvinism reflected the
autocratic societies which gave birth to it, while a government based on majority rule determined by elected representatives provided a different definition of human ability. HBS

was more convivial with religious beliefs granting free
choice to be a Christian rather than grace granted to a
chosen few.

Other evidence of the liberalization of Calvinism can
be seen in the easing of requirements for church membership.
Even after it rid itself of rebels such as Anne Hutchinson,
Roger Williams, and the Quaker Mary Dyer, the Puritan synthesis was falling apart. Since the young were not experiencing the saving conversion, the Half-Way Covenant was
adopted in 1662 to salvage what appeared to be a quickly
dissolving unity. The Half-Way Covenant permitted baptism
of the children of adults who had not undergone the conversion experience but who would "own the covenant" by promis-
ing to lead pious lives. Solomon Stoddard (d. 1718) took
the final step, offering access to the Lord's Supper and
even church membership in Northampton to anyone who would
abide by the moral code of the community.

HBS approved of the Half-Way Covenant, using Cotton
Mather's arguments to support her disagreement with Jonathan
Edwards' attempt to limit church membership and communion to
the elite group of saints who could prove a specific salvation
experience. She agreed with Mather that it was a "trouble-
some, dangerous underminer of reformation" to deny membership
to the children of the church members.[8]

In addition to the Puritan idea of a covenant between
God and the New Englanders, and the Puritan emendations of
Calvinist limitations of free will and church membership,
HBS adopted their views of the millenium and the importance
of family life. New England solemnity was alleviated by two
beliefs, both of which HBS embraced: one was the joyous
anticipation of the millenium, which spread a "rosy glow"
over the chosen people and their ministers who were "invariably a jolly set of fellows."[9] The other was the Hebraic
non-ascetic quality of Puritanism and its fascination with

the first chosen people and the first Zion of the Old Testament. Like the Jews, New England ministers and their people
felt that marriage was a holy state and that numerous children
were a blessing. Lyman Beecher was typical in having three
successive wives and fathering thirteen children. The
Puritans began "domesticating the Almighty" by making marriage a dominant metaphor for the interaction of God with man.
An example is an image used by Thomas Shepard: "The husband
is bound to bear with the wife, as being the weaker vessel;
and shall we think God will exempt himself from his own
rule?"[10]
        Idealization of the family was a major theme for Jonathan
Edwards, who stated that every family ought to be a little
church and that the family was a prime source of grace.[11]
It was to this Puritan emphasis on marriage and children
that HBS turned to for salvation.
        Although the Puritans were her heroes, she was critical
of some of their beliefs. Puritanism was a poor way to
raise children whose needs it ignored, as in the too rigorous
Sabbath observance. Her character Ellery Davenport (OTF)--
a duplicate of another character portrayed as Edwards'
grandson Aaron Burr (MW)--explained that Calvinism could
call forth the worst in a child: "Call a man a thief and
he'll steal."[12] As a boy Davenport felt free to lie and to
steal because he was told he could do nothing correctly
unless he received grace. But if he was saved, then all
would be forgiven. So he became a knave, a seducer and a
drunkard. Hopkinsian Calvinist Aunt Lois (OTF) told the
children in her household that there was no use in praying
if their hearts had not been changed. The melancholy dogma
of Calvinism taught that few were of the elect and that life
was a misfortune for the unsaved.
        What HBS and her father called "ultra-Calvinism" was
glacial, morbid severe, and appalling, like Nathaniel Emmons'

theology. It repressed emotion and self-expression, leaving only "dry husks of doctrinal catechism," a "literal famine of any aesthetic food."[13] Cold Puritan precision pressed those who could not accept its teaching to reject all religion.

Stowe then, with a fond glance back to the New England of Cotton Mather's *Magnalia*, glorified the Puritanism which flourished before the advent of Edwards and his tormenting theology. But she was even somewhat critical of that Golden Age, with its limitation of salvation to those who had a specific conversion experience and its neglect of earthly beauty and emotions. Covenant theology prevailed for only the first generation; it was dissolved by the emotionally exhausting soul-searching it demanded of its flocks, and by their new preoccupations with settling the frontier and a growing commerce. It was Edwards whom HBS blamed for the decline of Puritanism, and who seemed to haunt her through the pages of her books.

She wrote to Oliver Wendell Holmes, "I do not believe you or I can ever get the iron of Calvinism out of our souls,"[14] the strict soul searching of Puritans seeking for certainty of salvation. Her relationship to Calvinism was succinctly delineated by James Russell Lowell, the editor of the *Atlantic Monthly*, who wrote her:

> If, with your heart and brain, you are not orthodox, in Heaven's name who is? If you mean "Calvinistic," no woman could ever be such, for Calvinism is logic, and no woman worth the name could ever live by syllogisms. Woman charms a higher faculty in us than reason, God be praised.[15]

Feeling that "her people" were the orthodox, HBS would likely agree with Lowell's solution of the controversy. Her mistrust of masculine reason and "dry theology" and her praise of woman's self-sacrificing Christ-like love was the major theme of her writings.[16]

EDWARDS' FORMULA

Given her attitude towards Edwards, it is not surpris-
ing that many of her villains were either Edwardsian or
related to Edwards in some way. The wicked seducer characters Burr and Davenport were portrayed as his grandsons.
Padre Francesco *(Agnes)* with his concentration on God's
awful punishment of sinners, bruised the tender heart of a
woman. HBS saw both the monk and Edwards as preaching a God
of torture. Concerning Edwards she wrote her son Charles
that "some of his sermons are more terrible than Dante's
Hell...."[17]

She found Edwards' standards for regeneration too
difficult for the ordinary person. She viewed him as a
sublime thinker, a poet, the greatest theologian since
Augustine, and one who had climbed the great ladder of
salvation. But he had then cut away all the rungs for the
"feeble folks" whom he asked to follow him.[18]

Edwards' "rationalistic methods," HBS felt, undercut
the means for salvation, disrupted New England beliefs, and
led eventually to the Unitarian heresies of Emerson and
Parker. Parker/Edwards' theology made Christianity so
unobtainable for most people; the reaction against his
limitations on church membership led to the Unitarian lack
of theology and creed that HBS felt diluted Jesus' teachings.
She explained to her son Charles that Edwards' God "was not
a Father, not the God that Jesus meant when he said...he
that hath seen Me hath seen the Father."[19] Edwards reflected
an aristocratic, monarchical political system which was fast
disappearing in democratic America. His God, the most
powerful being in the universe, was "dispensed from all
obligation to seek anything but his own glory."[20] HBS
equated this view with the doctrine of divine right of
kings. She believed that the development of American democracy drew New England theology away from Edwards' teachings.

Chapter Two
A Rejection of the New England
Theology Salvation Formula

HBS was not a pioneer in the attack on Edwards; the women in her family led the way in shaping what her grandson Lyman called "the other gospel." Her mother Roxana dismissed the idea that disinterested love for God was the only real love. The second Mrs. Beecher silenced her husband's reading from *Sinners in the Hands of an Angry God*, considering it a "slander" to God's loving nature. Catharine wrote an able treatise refuting Edwards' concept of the will and affirming that if one sincerely tries then one will be saved. Lyman too suffered over Edwards' thought. When he became depressed by reading Edwards as a college student, Dwight advised Lyman that farmers harvest their crops rather than waiting for divine providence.[21]

Yet Edwards profoundly influenced HBS in his emphasis on the affections, for though a disciplined intellectual, it was the emotions Edwards sought to energize. He attacked the "extraordinary dullness in religion" which had carried over into the new century, saying that heads did not need to be filled but "hearts touched."[22] He attacked the rationalism emanating from Harvard, and rejected the formula of covenant theology. Out of his religion of the heart and his emphasis on sanctification sprang the great revivals.[23] Rather than relying on systematic preparation for salvation through knowledge of doctrine and pious living, the Awakening aimed to crack open the heart of the sinner. Edwards described to his congregation lucid portraits of heaven and hell, motivating them to prostrate themselves before God's mercy. His Northampton congregation responded vigorously, and was "never so full of love, nor so full of joy, and yet full of distress," he reported.

He defined true religion as "holy affections," and a "sense of the heart": his wife Sarah Pierpont was his prime example of the new sense in operation, and Abigail Hutchinson and young parishioner Phoebe Bartlet were others.[24] Using

the new Lockean psychology, Edwards explained that the
natural person is born without a sense or perception of the
supernatural nature of God's love. Adam had had that supernatural sense but as the head of mankind he lost it for all
of us in the Fall. People are wicked because they cannot
sense God's beauty, and therefore they love only themselves.
People have a natural ability to act with freedom but morally
are unable to will unselfishly since their motives are selfish. HBS, in contrast, believed this distinction between
natural ability and moral inability to be an absurd intellectual game and had one of her fictional preachers play the
fool as he tried to explain the distinction.[25]

     For Edwards, salvation occurs if God grants the opera-
tion of the new sense, the "relish" of pure beauty, excellence,
and benevolence that is God's being. Grace is not a mystical
infusion of a new nature but is a new ability to sense God,
rather like the ability of a formerly color-blind person to
distinguish colors. It motivates the will toward the love of
God and disinterested affection for his creation and away
from self-love.[26]

     HBS' rebellion against Edwards' attempt to confine
salvation to an elite was anticipated in his congregation's
rejection of his attempt to limit church membership and their
dismissal of him in 1750. "I won't worship a wig," (clergy
wore wigs) announced a young parishioner caught reading
"Granny books" with anatomy pictures.

     The leaven of success in conquering a virgin land was
potent, and Edwards was himself a party to the optimism which
became such a marked characteristic of the American faith:
he predicted that as a result of the Awakening the millenium
might well begin in America.

     HBS summed up her evaluation of Edwards thusly:

          Edwards fell into the error of making his own
          constitutional religious experience the
          measure and standard of all others, and

> revolutionizing by it the institutions of the
> Pilgrim Fathers....It was his power and his
> influence which succeeded in completely
> upsetting New England from the basis on which
> the Reformers and the Puritan Fathers had
> placed her, and casting out of the Church the
> children of the very saints and martyrs, who
> had come to this country for no other reason
> than to found a church.[27]

She did not concur that one had to have the new sense of
God's holiness in order to be saved, nor did she concur with
his view that one who was not converted was an enemy of God.

What she advocated instead was a theory of Christian
nurture such as that systematically developed by her contemporary Horace Bushnell.[28] She believed that a child "could
be raised up a Christian," a doctrine which she attributed
to the Cambridge Platform, to early Puritans and to Cotton
Mather. She quoted in agreement Mather's statement that it
was "a tyranny to impose upon every man a record of the
precise time and way of their conversion to God."[29] Through
love and the careful example of parents, a child could become
a good Christian without a specific conversion experience.
She avidly held that her own children who died before being
saved in the traditional manner--infant Charles, college
student Henry, alcoholic veteran Frederick, morphine-addicted
Georgiana--would one day greet her in heaven. She was nagged
by Calvinist doubts about their salvation, but dismissed
those doubts as the work of the devil. Furthermore, not only
could goodness be taught through parental love, but it could
perhaps also be inherited. It was her fervent hope that,
according to "the great law of descent," Christian generations
might gradually produce children more disposed to do good
than to do evil.[30] This was far removed from John Calvin and
Jonathan Edwards.

She believed that love and positive expectations were
the way to salvation, rather than Calvinist creeds and dogma.

Mr. Jekyll *(Dred)* was an example of the dangers of Edwards'
notions of true virtue: "He had slowly petrified into such a
steady consideration of the greatest general good, that he
was wholly inaccessible to any emotion of particular human-
ity."[31] She wished to turn away from the abstract thinking of
theologians to the concrete feelings of the individual.
Thus, though horrified by Edwards, HBS inherited his concern
for the heart, religious affections and sensibility, aesthetics and the importance of the family, in addition to his
glorification of New England. She also gained from the
legacy of the Great Awakening the confidence of the lay
person to speak his or her mind on religious issues and the
stress on inner experience and the Bible, rather than on
creed and doctrine. She also inherited the zeal for missionary reform activity which came with religious enthusiasm and
religion of the people.

THE CONSISTENT CALVINISTS' FORMULA

Through her father and her husband, she had not only to
face the ghost of Edwards but also those of his pupils.[32]
The Edwardsians banded together, calling themselves Consistent Calvinists, to distinguish themselves from the Old
Calvinists.[33] Both parties joined in opposition to Deists
and Unitarians.

The Old Calvinists believed that means were efficacious,
while the Consistent Calvinists held that they caused false
pride. The Old emphasized pragmatic action, while the New
were speculative thinkers. The Old had faith in human reason,
while the Consistent believed that it was corrupted by the
Fall. HBS' sympathies were with the Old Calvinists; she
was critical of the Consistents, especially singling out
Hopkins, who is fictionalized in *The Minister's Wooing*,
and Bellamy, whose *Nature of True Religion Delineated*
her character Horace's grandmother read every day *(OTF)*.

Emmons appeared as Dr. Stern in her autobiographical *Poganuc
People*. Let us look at these theologians as HBS saw them,
and then at Dwight and Taylor who were intimately associated
with Lyman Beecher in shaping the evangelical revivalism
which was her religious upbringing.

Joseph Bellamy (d. 1790) studied and lived with Edwards,
and joined with him in attacking the Half-Way Covenant. HBS
praised Bellamy as an "expert spiritual fisherman" and a
powerful preacher and theologian.[34] He sought to respond to
the rationalist critique of Calvinism that it made God the
author of sin and that it was unfair to damn great numbers of
humans who never had any opportunity to be saved. He replied
in a legalistic manner that God was just, a Moral Governor,
whose "vindictive justice" fairly punished sin.

Bellamy defined sin as selfishness: people are only
required to love God, but do not because of the "bad temper"
of their hearts. Sin is not a taint inherited from Adam but
is an inability to transcend self-love in favor of higher
love of God. People sin freely so they deserve punishment.
Bellamy preached that as "a proud, stubborn, guilty wretch;
you must come down first, and lie in the dust before the
Lord, and approve the law in the very bottom of your heart,
and own the sentence just by which you stand condemned."[35]
Bellamy expanded atonement to include all, not just limited
atonement for the elect, though sinners did not deserve it.
He also taught that it is necessary for the glory of God that
there be sin and the natural inability to earn salvation.
Without this impotence, the saved would not recognize God's
goodness in saving them from everlasting woe.

This vindictive Judge of a God who decrees that sin is
for the greatest good is not for the tender-hearted and HBS
was appalled. Her Consistent Calvinist-like priest, Fernando,
preached that "the Lord wills that His saints should come to
rejoice in the punishment of all heathens and heretics,"[36]

which was to HBS a cruel and barbaric view of God. She
painted Fernando as a warped and tormented personality.

Samuel Hopkins (d. 1803) was another close associate of
Edwards. HBS admired him for his pioneering and unpopular
abolitionist stand and for his emphasis on unselfishness.
She rejected, however, the harshness of his views; he system-
atized Consistent Calvinism. As the key phrase for Bellamy
was Moral Government, the key to Hopkins' system was Disinterested Benevolence. It had its origin in Edwards' concept of benevolence as the mark of the person with holy
affections. However, benevolence in Edwards' thought had a
greater implication of love, while to Bellamy it was a legalistic description of what the sinful man lacked.

Disinterested Benevolence is a term used by HBS in her
novels, as for example when she insisted that marriage was
consistent with that ideal. For Hopkins it meant that one is
so beyond self-love that she/he must be willing to be eter-
nally damned, if it would add to the glory of God. This was
his test of regeneration. His model for this unselfishness
was Sarah Edwards whom Hopkins heard state her resignation to
be damned if it were God's will. But HBS rejected Hopkins'
test of regeneration, as did her mother. (Lyman's response
to Hopkins' test of being willing to be damned for God's
glory was, "then, sir, you ought to be.")[37] One of her
female characters says very honestly, "I never could come to
it to say that I was willin' to be lost, if it was for the
glory of God."[38]

Hopkins did hold out some encouragement to work actively
toward salvation, although in a very convoluted way: one
must attempt to use the means of salvation, he said, because
if one is not making that attempt there is obviously no hope
of salvation. As the sinner has no taste for striving,
making an effort may be an indication of grace. Yet the
"awakened sinner" is more guilty in the eyes of God, perhaps

because she/he is guilty of thinking about his or her own
welfare. His prayers do no good and are an abomination to
God.[39] The individual was thus placed in a bind: if he was
not trying to be saved he was damned, but if he tried he
might be even more hateful in the eyes of God. The dilemma
is stated by Miss Mehitable *(OTF)*, who said that she sought
conversion,

> which our father taught us to expect as alchemists
> seek the philosopher's stone....The logical proofs
> of theology;--that God is my enemy, or that I am
> His; that every effort I make toward Him but
> aggravates my offense; and that this unknown gift
> which no child of Adam ever did compass of himself,
> is so completely in my own power, that I am every
> minute of my life to blame for not possessing it.[40]

Therefore man both should and should not work for salvation.[41]
Hopkins said, for example, that in "all his voluntary exer-
tions he is perfectly free and must be accountable." But
Hopkins also held that God was the cause of our volitions, so
the logic is rather difficult to ferret out.

Stowe raised objections to Hopkins through the character
Sam Lawson. Polly *(OTF)*, described as a great Hopkinsian,
was hard put to reply to Lawson's objection that, "ef a man's
cut off his hands it ain't to require him to chop wood," and
that if one is in a slippery well fifty feet deep one should
not be required to climb out unaided. Polly's response was
that "we did it [sinned] in Adam," for, as Edwards explained,
Adam was the representative federal head of mankind.

Hopkins believed in taking action once saved: regenerated,
a person was responsible for his or her own conversion through
"holy exercises." HBS shared this belief, and also agreed
with him that the number of those given a new heart would be
greater than those lost. Her spokeswoman Candace *(MW)*
believed that many more are saved than most people imagine.

In portraying Samuel Hopkins in *The Minister's Wooing*,
HBS felt free to alter facts of his life. Although the major

quality of both the real and the fictional Hopkins was
unselfishness. Stowe's Hopkins preached abolition in spite
of the opposition of powerful and important parishioners.
Most noble of all, he gave up his claims to his fiancée,
Mary, when her supposedly deceased sailor lover returned from
a voyage. In his actions Hopkins was both a kindly and brave
man. But his preaching only turned men like sailor James
Marvyn away from faith, and his doctrine was an "iron shroud"
to James' mother whom some view as a fictional Catharine.
Mary too was oppressed by her terror about the fate of her
unredeemed friends.

Stowe described the system of the fictional Hopkins as
abstract, narrow, cold with the "chills of analysis," dry and
unwieldy. Her Hopkins contradicted himself by preaching on
one Sunday that God is the "author of every act of will," and
then preaching free agency and total responsibility the
following Sunday. Like Edwards, his preaching of Disinterested Benevolence was so rarified that he "knocked out every
rung of the ladder [to heaven] but the highest."[42] He was a
noble man made ludicrous by his theology, which inflicted
great pain on women such as Mrs. Marvyn.

The third Consistent Calvinist that HBS portrayed was
Nathaniel Emmons, who is Dr. Stern in *Old Town Folks*.
Emmons had touched the life of the Beechers, not through
books, but through his sermons, which Catharine heard while
visiting the Fisher family after the death of her fiancé,
Alexander Fisher.[43] She rebelled against Emmons' insistence
on the conversion experience as necessary for entrance to
heaven, for Fisher had been as righteous and true as any man
could be, but he had not experienced saving grace. She
decided that justice decreed that an honorable and worthy
life did not deserve hellfire. She believed that Hopkins'
theology "made us mere machines, and all our wickedness was
put into us, and then we were required to be willing to be

miserable. It seemed to me that my lost friend had done all that unassisted human strength could do."[44] Catharine's rebellion was certainly a major catalyst in Harriet's rejection of Consistent Calvinism.

Emmons formulated what was called his "exercise" scheme. He taught that God is the sole causal agent and works through a chain of exercises to bring instant repentance; thus moral actions and deeds indicate regeneration: this has a distinct Hopkinsian flavor.

HBS' Dr. Stern preached that sin is the necessary means of the greatest good. The impact of his preaching was to drive young people from religion. They felt "revulsion against teachings which seem to accuse the great Father of all of the most frightful cruelty and injustice."[45] She praised him as being unworldly, but like Edwards and Hopkins, he had taken away the means of salvation from many. HBS echoed Catharine's perception: she described Stern as a "skillful engine of torture, to reproduce all the mental anguish of the most perfect sense of helplessness with the most torturing sense of responsibility."[46]

Emmons' exercise scheme was rejected by Timothy Dwight (d. 1817), who was more of a "taster," seeing regeneration as a change of heart. Yet Dwight was like Emmons in stressing action, doing, and making use of means. During his presidency and the revival he fomented, Yale students formed the Moral Society. This activism influenced Lyman and through him, Harriet. Dwight was keen in recognizing the impact of education and family status on morality. Lyman also had concern for the effect of external conditions on the soul. Harriet, in her turn, was careful to emphasize the impact of environment: she pointed out that if a child sleeps in a hot closed room he will be irritable. She suggested that a sermon on oxygen would perhaps "do more to repress sin than the most orthodox discourse."[47] She likewise saw the impact

of the mores of a given culture. Recognizing that poverty
was a damper on morality, she was especially provoked by the
treatment of beautiful girls, spoiled by men. About such a
woman, her character Lillie, she wrote that "if [she is]
much of a sinner, society has as much to answer for as she."[48]

THE NEW HAVEN FORMULA

Dwight's student, and Lyman Beecher's dearest colleague
throughout his ministerial career, Nathaniel Taylor (d. 1858),
affirmed a belief in depravity, election and the need for
atonement. However, "to what purpose," he asked, "do we
preach the gospel to men, if we cannot reach the conscience
with its charge of guilt and obligation to duty?"[49] He
found a way to expand hope for salvation. Using Scottish
Common Sense philosophy, Taylor deduced a neutral spot in
depraved man, which he called self-love.[50] This does not
mean selfishness, but the desire for happiness, which can be
realized only in God. The Holy Spirit acts on this neutral
point so that the sinner is drawn to the love of God. The
preacher can appeal to this principle of self-love, since
people have free moral agency and can act. It is the free
choice of some object other than God which constitutes depravity.

According to Taylor, it is certain that natural man will
choose to sin, because an infant is gratified according to
its selfish desires from the beginning when it cries and
receives its mother's breast. God could not prevent this
sinful behavior because he gave people freedom to choose;
Taylor rejected Bellamy's vision of sin as necessary or good
since it exists, believing that it is certain that man will
sin, although he has the power to do otherwise. He referred
to this concept, so central to his thinking, as "certainty
with power to the contrary," a phrase that appears consistently in his work.

Chapter Two
A Rejection of the New England
Theology Salvation Formula

Taylor and Beecher (d. 1863) carried Hopkins' subtle emphasis on the power of volition much further than Hopkins had.[51] The result was that the orthodox Consistent Calvinists accused the New Haven Divinity men of denying original sin, of limiting God's power, and of making the human being, rather than the Holy Spirit, the cause of regeneration.

The aim of Lyman Beecher's adult life was to foment the revivalist spirit, an aim which naturally found a target in his children, who felt the full weight of his energetic efforts to lead them to the light. He suffered over them, bewailing the fact that the children were all "stupid" and insensitive to the influence of the Holy Ghost. In spite of his worry, or perhaps because of it, they gradually fell in line, his sons becoming preachers, and his daughters, with the exception of Mary, active in reform movements.

The doctrinal contours of this paternal influence were largely cast in the mold of the New Haven theology of Nathaniel Taylor. Taylor placed great stress on the individual's responsibility for his sin. HBS explained that although her father believed in innate depravity, "yet practically he never seemed to realize that people were unbelievers for any reason than want of light."[52] In accordance with Bellamy's Moral Government theology, Lyman held that all people are moral agents, endowed with free will and the ability to choose salvation. God gives humans the ability to obey Biblical injunctions. Taylor and Beecher criticized Jonathan Edwards for limiting the sinner's natural ability, thus minimizing his or her responsibility for sin. Beecher called this limitation of human powers "entangling," stating that he, Lyman, was converted in spite of Edwards' books.

Taylor and Beecher believed that sin consists in sinning, that is, the violation of moral law entails a selfishness which must find fruition in specific acts before the individual can be held accountable. Depravity begins with account-

ability not with birth, thereby nullifying the Calvinist
doctrine of infant damnation and correlatively de-emphasiz-
ing the belief in original sin. The New Haven theologians
concerned primarily with revivals and spiritual metamorpho-
sis, recognized above all else the individual's power of
choice. Arminian in flavor, this perspective denied the
Calvinist position that natural man is utterly unable to work
toward salvation. Lyman was brought to trial in Ohio by Old
School Presbyterians in 1835 for denying original sin and the
inability of the sinner to save himself.

    Lyman attacked preachers who sat on "goose eggs of
imputation, inability and limited atonement" until the eggs
rotted under them.[53] He believed that the sinner is able to
choose salvation--which consists in loving God more than
himself/herself--but without saving grace he/she lacks the
willingness to effect this transcendence of pure self-interest.
God therefore does not rule by force but by motive. Man is
accountable because there is "such ability in man to do his
duty as constitutes him inexcusable, though God should never
make him willing to do it" [through the power of the Holy
Ghost to transmutate motive].[54]

    In instructing his children and congregations Lyman
further taught that the operation of the Holy Spirit is
usually closely associated with the use of means, which
include: reading the Bible, ceaseless prayer, confession of
sins and resolution to discontinue the ways of impiety,
seeking instruction, and a deep sense of one's own despicable
state of vileness--balanced by a belief in the universal
saving power of Christ's atonement, another modification of
Calvinism and its doctrine of limited atonement. In addition
he warned against too great a reliance on books and intellect,
stressing action and the emotions. If one availed him or
herself of the proper means, as elucidated in Lyman's "experi-
mental religion" and aroused by his preaching, in a week or

two the sinner should see the joyous results of election.

Unselfish benevolence and "vigorous action for God" were the credentials of the saved. Faith does not lead to salvation, he taught, unless it also leads to "good works." In this context the role of the revival was to provide more immediate access to the Godhead, for it was during the revival that the power of the Holy Ghost revealed itself most intensely, especially in the form of a heightened efficacy of means. When the revival faded God seemed a remote moral Governor whose concern was with justice and the carrying out of his laws, according to Catharine's report of her childhood.

Harriet, Catharine and Henry were major voices of their era: Harriet the most popular novelist, Henry the most popular preacher and Catharine an influential educator and founder of the study of Home Economics. They were stamped with their father's fiery revivalist commitment to save souls, and their ardor catapulted them into prominence under the Protestant banner of reform and the saving of America.

THE UNITARIAN NON-FORMULA

Neither Catharine nor Harriet turned to the Unitarian option of a God without vengeance or wrath. HBS was taught as a child that Unitarians were under the control of Satan in that they stood in the way of holy revival and conversion. Lyman went to Boston to wage war with the enemy, who he said were "as fire in my bones." He believed that their opposition to orthodoxy was one of the last controversies preceding the millenium. He catalogued their heresies: they divested Christianity of the supernatural, explained away regeneration, and did not acknowledge the reality of sin and reward or punishment in the after-life. HBS agreed that such a belief was an especially "dangerous" one. Finally, the Unitarians saw Calvinism only in caricature, not recognizing the truth

that men are depraved moral agents, accountable for sin, and
capable of being saved through Christ's atonement.

HBS was impressed by the literary achievements of
Unitarians and Transcendentalists, especially their magazines
The North American Review and *The Dial*. She told the Unitarian Oliver Wendell Holmes that she wholeheartedly supported the theology expressed in his novel *Elsie Venner*;
a critique of the doctrine of original sin, the novel concerns
the plight of a girl blighted by the effects of a rattlesnake
bite during her mother's pregnancy. She prized William
Ellery Channing for his "noble testimony" against slavery.
She shared Unitarian and Transcendental Romantic sympathies
and their reaction to the harshness of Calvinism, but she
found no meat in their theology. She refused to permit the
Atlantic to publish her *Old Town Folks*, as the magazine's
ridicule of the old Puritan ways was not to her liking.

She saw the Unitarians as a party of bitter protest, of
demolition rather than construction, of rejection of the
exclusive theocracy of the Puritans. The Unitarians were
united only in not believing in the Calvinism of the Puritans,
and were part of "a whole generation in the process of
reaction."[55] Although she could understand their positions,
she agreed with her father that they had no settled doctrines.
Her major criticism was that they lacked a positive system
of belief. In their lackluster theology, "God's law becomes
a piece of good advice...and God a good Father." She
explained to her son that he was a loving parent but he
sends "awful retribution" to follow violation of natural and
moral law.[56] Also, the Unitarian view of Christ as divine
but not deity was unappealing to her Christocentricity. She
was fearful and upset when her son Charles was attracted to
Unitarianism while a student at Harvard, warning him against
them as "a little band dissociated from the great body of
Christ's Church."[57]

In summary, HBS praised the New School theology of
Taylor and Beecher in contrast to Unitarianism or the medieval beliefs of "Scotch-Irish Presbyterian Calvinistic
fatalism." The New School theology was more rational,
recognized human free agency, and utilized modern non-
literal methods of Biblical interpretation. She urged the
use of the Baconian method of investigation of facts, asking
her husband Calvin to study regenerated people and facts,
instead of relying on catechisms and confessions of faith, as
she felt the Old School did.[58]

Harriet related to her children that she and their uncle
Henry believed that the old theology's moral government
emphasis defined a God of scorching wrath and in so doing
prevented one from being able to "get at his feelings or his
heart without some arrangements and machinery to get him
right." Preachers lacked the sympathy to understand God and
the simple religion which Christ taught, which was, "when you
sin your Father gives himself to you--himself to bear your
sorrows...." Instead of cold, dry technical systems, Harriet
and Henry advocated that "you grow large hearts," that one
undertands Christ by loving another more than oneself.[59]

HBS' INTERPRETATION OF PURITAN CONCEPTS

What then, in the light of HBS' desire for salvation for
all who were sincere, did she do with her Puritan inheritance,
a tradition which taught depravity, limited salvation to the
predestined elect, and assigned eternal damnation to the
masses? She maintained that her ideal was Puritanism--but
although she used their concepts and vocabulary in formu-
lating her own answers, she turned Calvinist Puritanism
upside down.

Stowe was never one to emphasize in depravity: dogs
were depraved, and "hes it hard," but that seemed about as
far as innate depravity went for HBS. If all was sin and

evil, why, she had a character to ask, would the world be so
beautiful and joyous? "If penance and toil were all we were
sent here for, why not make a world grim and desolate...?"[60]
She "nebber did eat dat ar' apple," said Candace (MW).
HBS argued that there was a higher nature slumbering in each
person which could be awakened with the proper environment.
One of her noble Christian women, Grace, spoke for HBS:

> "You will never make me believe...that there are
> any human beings absolutely without the capability
> of good. Steady patience and love and well-doing
> will at last tell upon any one. Consider how much
> your sex always do to weaken the moral sense of
> women, by liking and admiring them for being weak
> and foolish and inconsequent."[61]

But HBS was a realist, recognizing the downward gravita-
tion of worldly, materialistic, thoughtless humans who were
often animal-like in their lack of compassion. Read the
newspaper, she directed, to realize how wicked the world
is. The "unspiritual" are always the majority. She further
noted that "there is a sleeping tiger in the human breast
that delights in violence and blood."[62] This world is often
unendurable, filled with "illusions and shadows." Yet she
laid the blame for wickedness at the doorstep of the environment: the family, education, and society were the villains,
not Adam's sin. For example, beautiful women were often
spoiled by men, rather than by any innate depravity of their
own. Some of HBS' women were born angelic: believing in the
existence of Christ-like women who only want to love and
serve, she challenged: "we leave it entirely to theologians
to reconcile such facts with the theory of total depravity...."[63] She likely agreed with her sister Catharine that
innate depravity was a fiction of theology invented by Augustine.[64] Christ suffered for our sins, redeeming us through
his death, offering his grade to all who would accept it, she
taught.

HBS called upon the theory of pre-existence to help to
explain how people could be born virtuous. Her brothers
Edward and Charles had toyed with the notion as a means of
accounting for man's sinful nature; HBS turned it around,
attempting to elucidate the nature, not of sin, but virtue.
She drew support from Plato whom she quoted as saying that
"we all once had wings."[65] This reassuring and fairy tale
like concept appealed to one who called her heroines good
fairies. She believed that some beings, usually young girls,
are so pure that they have "spirit home-sickness--the dim
remembrance of a spirit once affiliated to some higher sphere,
of whose lost brightness all things fair are the vague remind-
ers. "[66] Thus she had no use for the notion of tabula rasa,
but spoke of innate predispositions. To her phrenology
indicated that people are born with certain natures, as her
brother Henry believed. One fictional example she provided
was Lillie who was born without much emotion, and who even
with the best of training would have been wanting in "the
loving power."[67]

In addition to an animal nature associated with nerves
and passion HBS maintained that each person had an immortal
spiritual nature. This higher nature is a bashful "heavenly
stranger," not at home in the world.[68] It is evoked by
loving nurture; it came even to spoiled Lillie because of the
unselfish love of her husband, and because of the purifica-
tion rendered through her suffering. The religious faculty
is unawakened and underdeveloped in most people--but it is
there to transform the beast at the kiss of an unselfish
lover who awakens it aided by divine grace.

HBS made the Puritan notion of depravity unrecognizable
to a Calvinist and did the same to the concept of a saintly
elite: broadening the idea, she found "the elect" in many
homes, in many countries, composed of "all good people in
every nation."[69] Neither did she restrict the channels of

salvation to any one denomination. For HBS the fundamental
requirement for salvation was sincere effort. The love of
Christ was like sunshine, available to all people, and thus
humans are not subject to a fixed, predetermined fate. She
taught that Jesus yearns to be received and patiently knocks
at the heart of each individual--"Nobody ever sincerely tried
to be a good man and failed."[70] As a proof of God's all-
embracing love, she consistently pointed to the Biblical
passage, "In my Father's House there are many mansions" (John
14:2).

     Though she defended predestination,[71] her view was
certainly not the orthodox concept. She wrote of a "particularly high Calvinist" who said it was clear that all was
decreed. A bystander replied, "You strong electioners think
you's among the elect! You wouldn't be so crank about it, if
you didn't! Now see here: if everything is decreed, how am
I going to help myself?"[72] Her view was that Christ designed
an ideal pattern for each of us, all different, and thus we
are born in his image "in embryo." But we have free will to
develop or not.[73]

     How was one to help oneself? Stowe's answer was to
transmute predestination into tender fatherly guidance which
is irresistible and radiates love. She taught her twins,
"You need the heart of a little child, to lean on your Heavenly
Father."[74] The question she raised was, if God was loving,
why then do good people suffer so intensely? Her answer was
that Providence gives both sorrow and joy for Christian
growth or "enlarging" through the "fires of affliction."
People learn by experience; thus she viewed her relationship
with Calvin, in many ways her opposite, as an opportunity for
him to learn to be "kind and considerate" and she to be
"systematic and regular."[75] Even Bolton, *(Wife)*, her character cursed with the demon alcohol, could believe that God
was "holding his hand," and that all would be rectified in

the afterlife. Another one of HBS' characters explained
that, "There is not one of the smallest of life's troubles
that has not been permitted by him; and permitted for specific
good purpose of the soul."[76]

Concerning the afterlife, HBS did retain the Puritan
belief in the Last Judgment, which could be viewed as fierce
and full of doom but she preferred to look at the other side,
as "the day of love."[77] She also defended the belief in the
resurrection of the physical body and awaited the coming of
the millenium. She was not sure about the form of the second
coming, "but whether visible or by the manifestation of the
Spirit, let us hasten and look forward to that final second
coming of our master, when the kingdoms of this world shall
be the kingdoms of our Lord...."[78]

In her eschatology she emphasized heaven with its
"dazzling ranks of angels" and assumed she would meet her
friends and family there. She explained that science recognized
the existence of other worlds and intelligences. She saw
notions of hellfire as a reflection of the influence of
Italian systems of "fiendish fires" for criminals requiring
punishment in the days of the early church.[79] She recognized
that Christ spoke of hell in "the most appalling language,"
as in his instructions to cut off one's right hand rather
than risk hell, but HBS defined it as existing in this life
as in sins of pride and self-will and in the lives of drunk-
ards and murderers. Punishment would follow the sinner to
the afterlife where "there is suffering, mysterious and
unutterably awful, the fruit of sin."[80]

In her Puritan realism she recognized the existence of
evil in the world and viewed it personified in the traditional figure of Satan, the Great Enemy who casts temptations
in one's path. For example, she warned Calvin to be cautious
of Satan's use of beautiful women to dazzle his senses and
"not to look or think too freely on womankind." She believed

that God somehow allowed Satan to reign in order to test our
willpower, telling her sister Mary that, "I don't think God
ever permitted the Devil to hatch a worse plot" than Henry's
adultery trial.[81]

But she told her readers that they had free will to
obtain the salvation freely offered by Christ. Satan is
present only when "called by the congenial indulgence of
wicked passions." Judas for instance was driven only by his
own wicked will: "to the last the love of God pursued him."[82]
She believed in evil spirits--"rulers of the darkness of this
world" and other invisible worlds--and suggested that part of
the torment of Christ's struggle in the garden of Gethsemane
was caused by "cruel and malignant spirits."[83]

She agonized, along with her siblings, over their father's
belief in eternal punishment. Her brother Charles wrote to
Henry in 1857 that eternal punishment was their father's main
idea, but asked, "yet Isabella and Mary, I fear, reject
father's belief on this point, and Hatty's mind is, I fear,
shaken--do you believe in it?"[84] She rejected endless punishment for past sins, but she accepted the

> eternal persistence in evil necessitating eternal
> punishment, since evil induces misery by the eternal
> nature of things.... It there any fair way of dis-
> posing of the current of assertion...without which
> one loses all faith in revelation, and throws us
> on pure naturalism? ...Of one thing I am sure,--
> probation does not end with this life, and the
> number of the redeemed may therefore be infinitely
> greater than the world's history leads us to
> suppose.[85]

In the future life people will grow to be "Kings and Priests
to God."[86]

She believed that it was vital to teach retribution if
people were to be induced to behave morally, and that clergy
erred in not teaching it for,

> if Christ meant nothing by his terribly plain words--
> or meant that everybody eventually and somehow or
> other would come out right--then his preaching, life
> and death was without point. God is love--salvation
> free--the spirit and the bride say come--but come
> you must or be lost.[87]

She thus retained the Puritan belief in reward and punishment
in the after-life, but rejected their salvation formula and
those of modifiers in the Edwards school of theology.

HBS naturally first sought for salvation in the tenets
of the New England theology of her childhood. She could not
obtain the required conviction of the justness of hellfire
earned by her sinful nature, since she was not given the
strength to perfect her nature--although she wanted to do so.
She therefore rejected much of New England theology. However,
her Puritan ancestry was dear to her and she sought links
with it through Cotton Mather, who wished to grant church
membership to all members' children. She blamed Jonathan
Edwards for altering the Puritan system, for knocking out all
the rungs of the ladder to salvation except the highest ones
of mystical conversion experience. She also blamed his
followers, such as Bellamy and Hopkins, for making theology
remote and salvation only for some while others should be
willing to be damned for the glory of God.

Although impressed by Unitarian urbane intellectuality,
it would have been anathema to embrace her father's enemy.
Furthermore, that denomination did not hold to the belief in
strict reward and punishment in the hereafter which she felt
was necessary to insure human morality. She turned instead
to the Episcopal practice of accepting as church members
those who were pious and faithful to church teachings. She
also rejected the harsh theology of clergymen and looked
instead to the loving nurture of motherly women.

NOTES

[1] Perry Miller and Thomas Johnson, *The Puritans*, (New York: Harper Torchbooks, 1963), V. 1, p. 297. See Appendix 2 for religious setting not fully discussed in this chapter.

[2] HBS to Charlie, 23 November 1879, from Scotland, Folder 213, Schlesinger Archives.

[3] Arminius was an early seventeenth century Dutch advocate of the belief in some human ability to work for salvation.

[4] HBS, *Old Town Folks*, V. L, (New York: AMS Press, 1967), first published in 1869, p. 23. Increase Mather (d. 1723) listed what sinners have the power to do, even though they may not choose to do so: observe the Sabbath, associate with good companions, read the Bible, stay awake during sermons, and ponder their sin and death. He preached, "Let them no more say, God must do all, we can do nothing" (Miller and Johnson, *The Puritans*, V. 1, p. 340).

[5] Perry Miller, *Nature's Nation* (Cambridge, Massachusetts: Belknap Press of Harvard University Press, 1967), p. 61.

[6] Ibid., p. 11.

[7] HBS, *Old Town Folks*, V. 2, p. 65.

[8] Ibid., V. 1, p. 415. She did not remind her readers, however, that Mather was an infant when the covenant was adopted, since he was her ideal representative of the New England Golden Age of noble and brave spirits who fought witches and Indians, and were recipients of special acts of Providence, as portrayed in Mather's *Magnalia Christi Americana*.

[9] Ibid., V. 2, p. 71.

[10] Edmund Morgan, *The Puritan Family*, (New York: Harper and Row, 1966), pp. 168, 48, 162.

[11]Elizabeth Dodds, *Marriage to a Difficult Man* (Philadelphia: Westminister Press, 1961), p. 54.

[12]HBS, *Old Town Folks*, V. 1, p. 360.

[13]HBS, *We and Our Neighbors*, p. 94.

[14]Henry May, introduction to *Old Town Folks*, p. 29 (no date provided by May).

[15]Charles Stowe, *Harriet Beecher Stowe*, letter written 2 April 1859, p. 335.

[16]HBS scholars disagree most about whether she was defending or attacking Calvinism. Charles Foster sees in her novel *The Minister's Wooing* her "final yes" to Calvinism, as embodied in the disinterested benevolence of the minister, Hopkins (Foster, *The Rungless Ladder*, p. 123). Henry May argued that HBS was too much in accord with the realism of Calvinism to discard it completely (Introduction to *Old Town Folks*, May, p. 20). However, her son Charles and her grandson Lyman Stowe, and scholars Edmund Wilson, Johanna Johnston, John Adams, and Alice Crozier viewed her novels as an attack on Calvinism as a "subtle poison." Barbara Cross believes that Lyman's children devised "strategies" to defeat his "intolerable God" (Cross, *Autobiography of Lyman Beecher*, V. 1, p. XIII).

[17]HBS to Charles, 4 May 1874, Mandrin, Florida, Folder 187, Schlesinger Archives.

[18]HBS, *Old Town Folks*, V. 2, p. 5. She saw the Half-Way Covenant's open membership and covenant theology as replacing the rungs on the ladder. She explained that God had made a compact with the Puritans and the seal was the baptism of the children of church members. Edwards accepted that but not membership or partaking of communion. Parrington believed that Edwards was HBS' hero, with Hopkins as her lesser saint, drawn by their "courageous rationalism" (Parrington, *The Romantic Revolution in America*, New York: Harcourt, Brace and Company, 1927, p. 373). However, it is precisely rationalism that she attacked.

[19]HBS to Charles, Mandrin, Florida, 4 May 1874, Folder 187, Schlesinger Archives.

[20]HBS, *Old Town Folks*, V. 1, p. 111.

[21]Lyman agreed that Edwards was overwhelming and "entangling" to common minds (Cross, *Autobiography of Lyman Beecher*,
V. 1, p. 29). His son Charles fell temporarily into the
"dark cloud" of fatalism due to reading Edwards, and this
reinforced the Beecher dread of Edwards. Calvin Stowe,
fellow Lane seminary professor, continued to describe himself
as an Edwardsian Calvinist, though he preached gentle sermons.

[22]Alan Heimert, *Religion and the American Mind*, (Cambridge, Mass.: Harvard University Press, 1966), p. 208.

[23]Precursors, or quickenings, had occurred in the 1720s
with the Tennents, father and sons, in New Jersey, and spread
throughout the colonies by the help of spellbinder George
Whitefield, who first came from England in 1738.

[24]Because of his intellectual bent Perry Miller main-
tains that he was not as sure of his heart's salvation as he
was sure of Sarah's. Others recognized this; he was told,
"They say your wife is going to heaven by a shorter route
than yourself" (Perry Miller, *Jonathan Edwards*, New York:
World Publishing Co., 1963, pp. 207-208). Stowe praised
Sarah as blessed with "saintly patience and unworldly elevation" that enabled her husband to withstand his troubles with
his Northampton congregation (HBS, *Poganuc People*, New York:
AMS Press, 1967, first published 1878, p. 180).

[25]HBS, *Poganuc People*, p. 11.

[26]The conversion of HBS' character Nina *(Dred)* is very
Edwardsian. Nina reported of her sense of Christ, "I have a
sense of him, his living and presence, that sometimes almost
overpowers me." She had loved the beauty of nature before,
but "it seems to me that I see something now in Jesus more
beautiful than all" *(Dred*, Vol. 1, p. 435).

[27]HBS, *Old Town Folks*, V. 1, p. 416.

[28]She only briefly mentioned Bushnell once in all the
writings perused by this author (in *Key to Uncle Tom's
Cabin)*. Alice Crozier is wrong when she suggested HBS did
not know of Bushnell. Bushnell, 1802-1876, was a liberal
Protestant, a graduate from Yale Divinity School and pastor

of a Congregational Church in Hartford. He taught Christian
nurture (so that conversion was a lifelong development) and
the symbolic nature of language, making literal Biblical
interpretation impossible. Another possible source for her
ideas about the importance of environment was Charles Dickens
who believed that HBS was influenced by him. His *Hard
Times*, published in 1854, illustrates the effect of upbringing on character. Tom and Louisa were doomed to tragic lives
because their father educated them with attention to facts
and rationality, without encouraging affect or imagination.
Sissy, raised in a lower class and economic status, but with
love and fancy, emerged as a happier loving person.

[29]HBS, *Old Town Folks*, V. 2, p. 82.

[30]Ibid., V. 1, p. 416.

[31]HBS, *Dred*, (New York: AMS Press, 1967, first published 1869), V. 1, p. 210.

[32]Generally the genealogy of New England theology is
traced from Edwards to Bellamy and Hopkins to Dwight to
Taylor and Beecher. However, Sidney Mead, in his work on
Taylor, believed that a more accurate genealogy connects
Dwight with the Old Calvinists, bypassing the Edwardsians.
Mead found the Old and Consistent Calvinists distinguished by
disagreement about means, metaphysics, reason, and self-love,
Mead seeing Dwight and his pupils in line with the Old Cal-
vinist positions. (Mead, *Nathaniel Taylor*, p. 123).

[33]The New or Consistent Calvinists were a travesty on
Edwards and Calvin, according to Hartounian in his *Piety Versus Moralism* (Hamden, Conn.: Archon Books, 1964). He finds
that they were legalistic and moralistic in their emphasis on
the moral government of God, leaving out the mystical qualities of his grace and love.

[34]HBS, *The Mayflower* in *The Writings of Harriet Beecher
Stowe*, Vol. XIV, (Cambridge, Mass.: Houghton, Mifflin,
1896), p. 227.

[35]Joseph Bellamy, *True Religion Delineated*, (American
Antiquarian Society, 1969, microcard 6462, p. 27; originally
published Boston: Kreeland, 1750.)

[36]HBS, *Agnes of Sorrento*, (New York: AMS Press, 1967,
first published 1862), p. 67.

[37]Stuart Henry, *Unvanquished Puritan*, p. 108.

[38]HBS, *The Minister's Wooing*, p. 254.

[39]This emphasis on passivity was in line with Federalist
wishes for the quietude of the populace, according to Heimert
(Heimert, *Religion and the American Mind*, p. 499).

[40]HBS, *Old Town Folks*, V. 1, p. 248.

[41]Foster explained that Hopkins put more emphasis on the
power of the will to perform moral acts than Edwards did;
Edwards put liberty in physical freedom while Hopkins put it
in volition (Foster, *The Rungless Ladder*, p. 166).

[42]HBS, *The Minister's Wooing*, p. 88.

[43]Emmons preached in his funeral sermon that Fisher's
death "may have a happy effect upon a very sensible and
highly accomplished young lady" by awakening her to the need
for salvation. He also encouraged his listeners to believe
that there was "some ground to hope that he had experienced a
saving change." (Jacob Ide, ed., *The Work of Nathaniel
Emmons*, Vol. III: Boston, 1842, pps. 258, 259).

[44]Harveston, *Catharine Beecher: Pioneer Educator*,
letter 1 January 1823, p. 366.

[45]HBS, *Old Town Folks*, Vol. 1, p. 442.

[46]Ibid., p. 434.

[47]HBS, *Household Papers and Stories*, (New York: AMS
Press, 1967, first published in 1864 and in *The Atlantic
Monthly* as *House and Home Papers* and *The Chimney Corner*),
p. 192.

[48]HBS, *Pink and White Tyranny*, p. 51.

[49]Sidney Alstrom, ed., *Theology in America: The Major
Protestant Voices*, (New York: Bobbs-Merrill Co., 1967), p.
239. From Taylor's *Concio ad Clerum*, 1828.

[50]HBS reported that Lyman regarded the Scotch philosophy as only partially true. (*Men of Our Times*, p. 536).

[51]Sidney Mead saw that Taylor and Beecher had traveled far from the Calvinist Edwardsian fold. Mead disagreed with Foster's analysis that to concur with Edwards was their "highest ambition" (Charles Foster, *The Rungless Ladder*, p. 365). Mead believed that they were forced to return to Calvinism, in name only, by the controversy with the Boston Unitarians. The result was that "the forced marriage with Calvinism verged on incomprehensibility" (Mead, *Nathaniel Taylor*, p. 127).

[52]Barbara Cross, ed., *The Autobiography of Lyman Beecher*, V. 1, p. 394.

[53]Stuart Henry, *The Unvanquished Puritan*, p. 250.

[54]Barbara Cross, ed., *The Autobiography of Lyman Beecher*, V. 1, p. 143.

[55]Ibid., V. 2, p. 81.

[56]HBS to Charles, 7 March 1879, Mandrin, Florida, Folder 196, Schlesinger Archives.

[57]HBS to Charles, 5 March 1880, Folder 216, Schlesinger Archives. See Appendix 2 for her account of The Unitarian Controversy.

[58]HBS, to her family, 15 July 1844, Indianapolis, Folder 69, Schlesinger Archives.

[59]HBS to the twins, 8 March 1859, Brooklyn, Folder 103, Schlesinger Archives. McCray reported that contemporaries noted Stowe's impact on strengthening the "Liberal, evangelical party of New England." (*The Life Work of the Author of Uncle Tom's Cabin*, p. 255.)

[60]HBS, *Agnes of Sorrento*, p. 230.

[61]HBS, *Pink and White Tyranny*, pp. 316-317.

[62]HBS, *Dred*, V. 2, p. 152.

[63]HBS, *The Pearl of Orr's Island* (New York: AMS Press,
1967, first published 1862), p. 100.

[64]Harveston, *Catharine Beecher: Pioneer Educator,*
p. 158.

[65]HBS, *Old Town Folks,* V. 2, p. 88.

[66]HBS, *The Pearl of Orr's Island,* p. 296. Dickens also
wrote of Esther Summerson as a good fairy in *Bleak House*
(1864).

[67]HBS, *Pink and White Tyranny,* p. 324.

[68]Ibid., p. 63.

[69]HBS, *Old Town Folks,* V. 1, p. 375. She did distinguish between two classes of people: "One seems made to give
love, and the other to take it (*Pearl,* p. 102)," the former
are usually women and the latter often men. Mara and Moses
(*Pearl*) are the epitome of the two kinds of people--Moses
wanted Mara to work and pray for him and she wanted desper-
ately to save him, which she finally did.

[70]HBS, *My Wife and I,* p. 49.

[71]At least according to Charles Foster (*The Rungless
Ladder,* p. 101).

[72]HBS, *Dred,* V. 1, p. 320.

[73]HBS, 1 June 1874, Folder 115, p. 2, Schlesinger
Archives.

[74]HBS to Hattie, 4 March 1859, Brooklyn, Folder 103,
Schlesinger Archives.

[75]HBS to Calvin, 2 January 1847, Boston, Folder 72,
Schlesinger Archives.

[76]HBS, *Old Town Folks,* V. 1, p. 292.

[77]HBS, *The Pearl of Orr's Island,* p. 383.

[78]HBS, *Religious Studies and Poems*, (New York: AMS
Press, 1967), p. 182.

[79]HBS, *Agnes of Sorrento*, p. 69.

[80]HBS to Charlie, 2 April 1881, Mandrin, Florida, Folder
223, Schlesinger Archives.

[81]HBS to Calvin, 19 July 1844, Indiana, Folder 69,
Schlesinger Archives.   HBS to Mary Perkins, 15 January 1875,
Mandrin, Florida, Folder 99.

[82]HBS, *Religious Sketches*, p. 148.

[83]Ibid., p. 164.

[84]Sklar, *Catharine Beecher*, p. 231.

[85]Charles Stowe, *Harriet Beecher Stowe*, p. 340 (30 June
1858 to Lady Byron).

[86]HBS to Charlie, 20 March 1881, Mandrin, Folder 222,
Schlesinger Archives.

[87]HBS to Charlie, 7 March 1879, Mandrin, Folder 196,
Schlesinger Archives.

CHAPTER THREE
Salvation Found in Womanhood

HBS' FORMULA

Replacing the Puritan salvation formulation with her
own, HBS stressed the necessity of suffering, human love,
childlike simplicity, and Bible study with "heart consciousness." These comprised the sure path to salvation, a liberation which found its stamp in the performance of works for
the good of others. All these requirements were matched best ⅄
by woman's nature, as her heroines illustrated.

Without suffering and trials one remains shallow and
unawakened: The Arminian Parson Lothrop's (OTF) life was so
peaceful and "unruffled" that he had no depth; Tina's (OTF)
religious qualities were as underdeveloped as a robin's until
she suffered in her marriage to wicked Elery Davenport; and
children of difficult parents, e.g. a drunk father and an
invalid mother, gained in virtue. The death of a loved
woman, usually a pure young girl, was often efficacious, for
the suffering it caused deepened the mourner. Thus she
explained that sorrow is the "seed-bed where the plants of
the higher life strike deepest root,"[1] but if one is left to
suffer without guidance and love, she/he is lost. A child
surrounded by the "fierce goblin lineaments" of evil influences finds that "all is over with him forever."[2] Christ's
care for people is the only antidote: through earthly voices
and human hands Jesus speaks the language of love and concern.
HBS asserts, "All the good in the world is done by the personality of people.[3]

Maggie (Neighbors) provides an example of the impact of
an evil environment. A beautiful Irish girl, she was spoiled
by her parents, who made a plaything of her; later, working
for a woman who was critical and harping further frayed her

moral fabric. All this finally contributed to her suffering
a degrading seduction which could have been prevented, HBS
observed, had Maggie's employer shown "motherly care and
sympathy."

     But hope remained--for Christ came to save the lost
sheep. Maggie's salvation was effected through love. A
subsequent employer, _Eva_, was aided in her efforts by heavenly angels who enabled her to say and do what was needed.
Prayers, soothing hymns, and an opportunity for employment as
well as loving concern and forgiveness saved Maggie from
prostitution, and in reciprocating human love, Maggie's
affection and gratitude grew into love for Jesus.

     Because caring and loving assumed such importance, HBS
recognized the necessity of having a good mother. Indeed,
the power of the mother was such that it was not imperative
that she be living; HBS suggested that a deceased mother like
her own could perhaps do even more good than a living one. A
heavenly mother could conduct her ministry above "the tempests
and tossings of life."[4] To illustrate this, Harry _(OTF)_
was guided by his dead mother, whose spirit the clairvoyant
Horace was able to see hovering around her son, and benefited
from her intercession as when she stopped a drunk man from
striking him. In this manner she believed that the dead pull
the living toward heaven with "an invisible chain of love."[5]

     A mother, a wife, a young girl did the most pulling,
especially on men. She quoted Goethe's famous "eternal
womanly draws upward and onward," and contended that women
are in some way "the first or last cause of everything that
is going on."[6] This transforming ability is the defining
power of HBS' heroines, who evoke the higher nature of lovers,
fathers, sons, and neighbors. They also had the power to be
corruptors and destroyers of men if not educated properly,
she noted.

The male in return summons and rescues the female. For
example, Nina and Lillie were saved by their lovers, although
these men were guided by their strong pious sisters. But men
are less able to be transformational because according to her
character Harry, "we men have much more to contend with, in
the pride of our nature, in our habits of worldly reasoning.
It takes us long to learn the lesson that faith is the highest wisdom."[7] Women have another asset, their beauty, which
is a means of grace, drawing men toward heaven: "a beautiful
face is a kind of psalm which makes one want to be good."[8]
Thus, except for the spinsters, HBS' heroines are invariably
lovely.

The qualities HBS considered requisite for salvation
were to be intuitive, emotional and excelling in heart rather
than head; here it is obvious that the Christian injunction
to "become as little children" may be paraphrased as "become
as women." HBS was herself described as childlike and
"swayed and ruled by her affections;" as one of her twin
daughters described her, Harriet was her "little mother,
smiling happily, unconscious as a child."[9] HBS' heroines
were often called "child" by their men. A child trusts,
plays, smiles: a child does not ponder abstractions. One of
the few really heroic male ministers found in Stowe's novels
had "almost childlike simplicity...wholly devoid of any
ecclesiastical wisdom."[10] This was her ideal, and woman's
nature was of this essence. Women were often defined as
innocent and naive like children and romantics praised the
virtues of childlike simplicity unjaded by civilization.
Woman/child/nature/goodness were often viewed as similar and
the prototype of Christ's injunction to become like children.

Affinity with nature is another aspect shared by the
woman and child stereotypes. According to both HBS and her
brother Henry, contact with God's creation refines and brings

one closer to God. Her heroines all reflected her love of
flowers and adorned themselves with them: thus they were
both images of and paths to the power of natural beauty.

Both HBS and Lyman believed in childlike joy, considering it a mark of the saved. An example of her spirit of fun
occurred when Calvin was upset that she had cooked eggs he
had meant for brood hens. When he came home from work, he
found his wife, the children and their dog in the hen house,
sitting on a beam, cackling, as replacements for his lost
chicks.

In order to be saved, in addition to suffering, having a
good mother, and being childlike, one must study the Bible.
One must know it with the "deep heart consciousness" which
intuitively realizes the Bible to be the living truth. As a
source of spiritual power to seekers, HBS felt that it contains the solution to all problems. It has an enchanted
healing power. Even a dry list of genealogies was a "sacred
charm, an amulet of peace" to her character Mary Higgins.
Though it was not necessary to accept every word literally
since the Bible was written in "images and metaphors,"[11] it
was necessary to read it often and partake of its sacred
presence.

The most potent means of salvation is the love of Christ.
In convincing others of Christ's love one participated in the
work of salvation: "Once penetrate any human soul with the
full belief that God loves him, and you save him."[12] This
was exactly how the child Dolly (HBS' fictional self) saved
gruff Zeph Higgins. During a revival she asked him, "Don't
you know that Christ loves you?... Only trust him. You will
trust him." Her positive approach worked; Zeph yielded his
will and said, "I will," and was saved.[13]

As HBS' grandson Lyman noted, all of Beecher's children
were "Christ-worshippers"--the phrase was Harriet's.[14] She
kept a crucifix over her bed in Andover as a visible sign of

His presence. Jesus, her Friend and Elder Brother, was the
solution to her "disease of thought" and her torments with
the New England salvation formula. Nina, one of her spokespersons (Dred), was quizzed about her beliefs--did she love
God for His holiness and not because of His love for her?
And did she view sin as infinite evil? Nina replied that she
thought only of the beauty of Christ. She, like HBS, lacked
the infinite sense of sin. What Stowe saw as necessary for
salvation was to love Jesus and to do good.

This emphasis on nonrational means led naturally to the
avoidance of "ontological algebra" and the "harsh hands of
metaphysical analysis." There was not a bit of theology in
the Sermon on the Mount, she contended. One needs only to
study the life of Christ. She rejected "the tyranny of mere
logical methods," viewing logic as sterile, speculative,
severe and morbid. Through her character Eva, she advocated
another way: "Let's not act reasonably, let's act by something higher." [15] Doctrine and "metaphysical hairsplitting"
drove young people from the churches, she explained, which
should instead offer them amusing activities.

She identified theology with masculine dominance of
religion. She asserted that "Women's nature has never been
consulted in theology." Having its origins in men such as
Augustine, who, she believed, was ignorant of woman, theology
considered woman "only in her animal nature as a temptation
and a snare." [16] The church fathers defined woman as made
from man's rib to be his helper and procreator. Only in
conjunction with a man could a woman reflect God's full
image, according to Augustine. Women particularly shared in
Eve's sin. Aquinas taught that in the conception of an
embryo, the woman provides the flesh and the man the spirit.
Women are more tied to nature, more carnal in their appetites
as the witchcraft trials concluded, while men aspire more to
spiritual heights. HBS rejected the church fathers'

denigration of female spirituality. Because of this misogy-
nist cast of theology, women found it harder to tolerate or
assimilate its conflicts, many being ruined in the process,
she noted.

Ministers and the denominations they represented were
impediments to salvation.[17] Her Edward Clayton found that
preaching weakened his faith (Dred). Ministers were alienating in that some were motivated, not by the love of Christ,
but by intellectual concern about "-ion" words (such as
dispensation, sanctification, edification), by concern about
self-display and oratory, and by desire to make their denomination more powerful.

Stowe's character Uncle Tiff noted that the Presbyterians, Methodists, Episcopalians, and Baptists were "all a-
blowing out at each other," and wondered if that was the way
to Canaan. Her answer was an emphatic "No!" There is more
religion in the hearts of honest lay people "than is plas-
tered up behind the white cravat of clergymen."[18] None of
her ministers were responsible for the salvation of major
characters--this was accomplished by a lover, a child, a
mother or a sister. In her "secularized gospel,"[19] that is,
her placing salvation's locus in the home rather than the
church, HBS preached that LOVE was the means of grace, the
greatest earthly sacrament.[20]

Though she was bitter about ministers and their preoccupation with theological hairsplitting, when they were
attacked--as by Frederick Douglas--she defended them. She
averred that she was the daughter, sister, wife (and later,
mother) of ministers, and that churchgoers were the best
people in America and churches the highest form of social
organization. But she maintained that the true Christian
Church was composed of good people everywhere, living and
dead joined in the body of the invisible church--not just in
denominations.

Apart from her distaste for theological infighting, HBS
concurred with the Pauline and Puritan view of the need to be
a new person in Christ, the necessity for spiritual transformation of one's original nature. For example, the "natural"
Lillie *(PWT)* was selfish, vain, and dishonest. She smoked,
painted her face, read French novels, was not a good mother,
flirted with men after her marriage, and almost had an adul-
terous affair in which she was the aggressor. These traits
were a catalogue of what HBS most despised in women. But
even Lillie was saved before she died. She might have been
saved much earlier if she had not been spoiled by men or if
she had married the man she truly loved, despite his lack of
wealth. Over the period of a year she felt the "coming in of
a soul." It was accompanied by a feeling whose newness made
her irritable--yet she died knowing that she would join her
husband in heaven.

Nina *(Dred)* also felt a soul coming in. Previously,
while "her deeper part still slept," she was willful and
selfish. Yet the love of her fiancé, her reading the Bible
to a poor family, and the suffering she endured in nursing
the sick during a cholera epidemic all served to awaken her
soul. In a similar way, generated by her love of Agostino,
"a mysterious new inner birth" also came to Agnes. Another
young woman in love was also redeemed so that "the undine had
received a soul and was a true woman." [21]

For HBS the awakening of the higher nature is best
accomplished by the domestic enactment of Christ's unselfish
love and union with humankind--marriage and motherhood. The
stage for marriage is the home, and women are the hubs of
their homes. In this way they are pivotal to salvation, for
their natures are more refined and pure than men's and they
are not confined by the limitations of intellect.

She urged that action must ensue upon the awakening of
the soul: it is better for a woman to be making dolls for
poor children than to be an ascetic praying in the desert.
The saved must seek "to save the lost." She stressed doing
rather than thinking. Her Candace established the standard
for a good person: "generate or unregenerate, it's all one
to me. I believe a man dat <u>acts</u>.... Him as stands up for
the poor--he's my man."[22]

With acceptance of Christ the final seal of salvation is
vision of the Lord after death. "Death shall change him into
all that is enlightened, wise, and refined, for he shall
awake in 'His' likeness."[23] Sin will be taken away forever.
It is not clear how this fits into her belief in continued
probation after death, unless probation is necessary only for
those who did not accept Christ in this life. She maintained
that in Heaven one's personality would continue to grow and
"unfold in new and more beautiful forms."[24]

HBS' WOMEN AS SAVIORS

In every novel she wrote HBS preached reverence for
women. She frequently described them with these terms:
angel, priestess, sibyl, madonna, saintly, household goddesses and fairies. In <u>Uncle Tom's Cabin</u>, Eva was painted as
an angelic savior; her grandmother St. Clare was a "direct
embodiment and personification of the New Testament;" Mrs.
Shelby and Mrs. Bird were the moral force of conscience in
their families; and Eliza's "gentler spirit" guided her
husband. In <u>Dred</u>, Nina was revered by her half-brother Harry
and was the model of Christian faith for her intellectual
fiancé, who said that she should be his spiritual director.
The slave Milly was a Christian pacifist whose words re-
strained Dred from a violent uprising. In <u>My Wife and I</u>
and <u>We and Our Neighbors</u>, Eva wanted a man who would worship

her, and she got one. Her husband explained that she was
inspiring and beautiful, asking, "Why shouldn't I worship at
her shrine and cherish her image as Dante did that of Beatrice...?" He adored her with the devotion one gives to all
beauty, he said.[25] These examples can be multiplied.[26]

Harriet drew from Catharine's ideology of female domesticity that was grounded on the central tenet of self-sacrifi-
cial service to others as a major requisite of virtue and as
leading to female self-fulfillment.[27] She defined moral
leadership as characterized by loving self-sacrifice, thus
giving women moral superiority and displacing the Consistent
Calvinist theme of Disinterested Benevolence. Women were
required to give up satisfaction of personal needs in order
to accommodate and mediate those of a father, husband, or a
male-oriented society. Catharine encouraged this unselfish
submissiveness as the means by which to prevent too much
competitiveness and divisiveness in the nation. Instead of
facing class, ethnic or regional conflicts she divided
society into male and female and asked the latter to serve
the former, as subordinate to superior, in divinely ordained
roles. If women were ambitious for power, they would lose
the security offered by men trained in chivalry and gallantry. She wanted spiritual power for women rather than
political power. Her techniques were different than feminists;
instead of working for women's suffrage she thought women had
more avenues open to them by piously influencing children and
husbands. In their acceptance of subordination women became
redemptive, as was Christ's sacrificial death.

From the 1830s on Catharine reattributed moral leadership not to male clergy, but to female laity in their domestic
roles as mother, nurse and teacher. She believed that the
theories of morality and religion "are especially to be
examined and decided on by woman, as the heaven-appointed
educator of infancy and childhood."[28] She said that no queen

stood in a more exalted position than a mother. She advocated that women bring Christianity to the West by serving as
school teachers in western communities where a center would
form first around a school rather than a church. She attempted
to put her plan into action and did succeed in sending over
five hundred single women into the West as teachers. However, she believed that for the most part women should marry
and stay close to home. In her praise of woman's unselfishness and saving powers as mother, nurse, and teacher, she
provided a female alternative to male domination of the
church. She urged clergy to teach more to women for they
were under the moral obligation to use all available talent
to help save a "perishing world."

Why were women so saintly? First, Stowe explained that
they did not have the sexual temptations that men had; HBS
took her own case to be the norm, writing to Calvin that she
had no sexual passion and therefore felt no jealousy; yet she
sympathized with his male temptations, sparked by beautiful
young women.[29] She asserted the chaste purity of woman,
contrasting it with the baser male inclinations, and identi-
fying men with the physical body and women with the spirit.[30]

Women's bodies and minds are made of "finer clay, nicer
perceptions, refined fibre." Their nervous systems are more
intense, sensitive, magnetic, mysterious, intuitive and
prophetic. Not encumbered by slavery to intellect, their
instincts are sharper: they are soul-artists, characterized
by acute perceptions which surpass "slow-footed reason."
They are also skilled in tactfulness and the "power of charm-
ing." Women of this caliber are "God's real priests," not
male ministers mired in dogma.[31] HBS perhaps saw herself as
one of the real priests; she believed that she was chosen as
God's instrument to write *Uncle Tom's Cabin*.

This complementary male-female relationship was capable
of fostering a sort of soul cooperation; the outstanding

paradigm of it was Jonathan Edwards who she believed depended
on Sarah for spiritual inspiration. The model was repeated
in the marriages of Lyman and Roxana Beecher and Calvin and
Harriet Stowe. When Calvin was away from home with the
"hypos" he relied upon her letters to renew his faith, writing to her, "I have felt that I could have some hold on
Christ through you," since Harriet had the spirit of "life
which you are capable of giving and I am not."[32] Like her
heroines she was small, gentle yet powerful, the inspiration
of her family--the dominant spiritual force.

HBS believed that the most sacred earthly love is for
the "dear silver-haired angels, who seem to form the con-
necting link between heaven and earth."[33] Motherhood was
essentially holy, relating to the manifestation of Christ's
love and selflessness; it was a fount of spiritual grace to
her family, just as Mary's conception of Jesus was a source
of spiritual salvation for mankind. HBS cited the Genesis
passage predicting that the seed of woman would bruise the
serpent to glorify both Mary and womankind.

Mothers are entrusted with the duties and powers of
education, love, redemption and divination. For this reason
she dwelt upon the impact of the mothers of her *Men of Our
Times*. She explained that mothers had a mediating power; as
one of her male characters said, "Mother, if I ever get to
heaven it will be through you."[34] This was a spiritual basis
for her political support of women's suffrage: with the vote
women had a means of spreading their beneficial influence
over the whole nation. "Motherly" was one of her highest
words of praise: she used it to describe Jesus, Cotton
Mather, the Bible, and New England churches.

In her Protestant Mariology, HBS stressed the role of
the mother of Jesus, "the greatest archetype of Christian
motherhood."[35] If raised a Catholic, HBS would have been

ardently devoted to the Holy Mother. Protestants retained no
female images of the divine since they disregarded Mary as a
cult figure. Stowe risked raised eyebrows when she hung four
pictures of the Virgin on the walls of her Hartford home.
She praised Mary as much as possible in a milieu that looked
askance at Mary worship. In fact, since Mary was the only
earthly parent of Jesus, she concluded that he had more of
the feminine than any other man. HBS spoke of Mary as the
teacher of Jesus, neglecting mention of Joseph. Mary was
also more insightful than the disciples, HBS noted, knowing
more calmly and clearly what Christ's purpose was and she
stood by him at the cross when his male disciples had deser-
ted him. HBS called Mary a blessed priestess, a poetess, an
inspirational bright star in heaven, and "the crowned queen
of woman." Mary was quiet, like Roxana; indeed, in many ways
HBS' view of Mary and of her secular madonnas seems modeled
on Roxana. [36]

Other Biblical women inhabited her pantheon: she pointed
to the strength of Sarah, Deborah, Huldah, Vashti, and Anna
as well as of Greek and Roman goddesses. She reminded her
readers that the house of Lazareth and his sisters was
referred to as Martha's and she reiterated the passage in
Acts which states that women shall prophesy. She also noted
the church work of deaconesses.

She adapted Paul for her own purposes: since a man was
supposed to instruct his wife he should stop reading his
newspaper to answer her questions; and since he was supposed
to be her head and protector he should be at least equal in
moral purity. She believed that Paul's allusions to women
praying and giving prophecy in public were not meant to
prohibit those activities but rather to make sure they were
accomplished with "female delicacy." [37] But she had reservations about Paul, thinking him outdated. Modern times were

different: married partners should make decisions together,
sharing responsibility as they shared love. She was against
male self-will and female servility. She countered Paul with
Genesis: like Adam, who took the apple from Eve, men have
both obeyed women and used them as scapegoats, thus diminish-
ing much of their salutary power, a power HBS saw demonstrat-
ed in the preaching of some of her contemporary women evangelists. She did not believe, however, that many women would
be called to public ministries; most would stay close to
home.

    Her admiration for Quaker women preachers, such as the
Englishwoman Sybil Jones, and for other religious leaders
such as the pietist Madame Guyon, found expression in her
portrait of Dolly (PP), whose preaching proved quite effective as in converting stubborn Zeph. Her character Eva
became the "little mother no less than wife," to her husband
(Wife), thus demonstrating another aspect of the female
potency for without a good mother and wife a man is lost.
"We all need the motherly, and we must find it in a wife" who
guides, cares for, teaches, and catechises her husband.[38]

    HBS contributed to some degree in what Fiedler has
called the American castration of the father.[39] A husband
she playfully defined as a tame "pleasant domestic animal"
who obeyed his wife,[40] requiring the guidance of the household priestess. Like her sister Catharine, HBS believed that
the woman was the minister of the family. Not only do husbands need motherly wives for such practical things as
managing the home, but also for spiritual fulfillment for
marriage is itself a sacred and holy sacrament, generating
grace. She believed marriage was a symbolic model for union
with Christ. This was why God told Adam that it was not good
for him to be alone: he needed a spiritual complement. Thus
Stowe believed, for example, that a steady person will marry

a volatile one to maintain a balance. In addition, the
wife's function was both to represent and to call forth her
husband's higher self: as priestess of the home, she was the
effective agent for her husband's spiritual rebirth.

Together man and wife learn the lessons of selflessness
in rearing their children; hence in such things as staying up
at night with sick children the husband and wife share in
spiritual edification. These exercises in gracious giving
are the "last and highest finish that earth can put on them,"[41]
for HBS saw marriage as conducive to universal benevolence
and the fulfillment of the purpose of the human soul.

For HBS the home in many ways was a kind of church. The
home offered avenues for unselfish action, symbolized union
with Christ, embodied love, and in its physical beauty,
refined the soul. Families should beautify the home with
plants, flowers, inexpensive prints, a cheery fireplace, and
colorful wall paper.[42] In accordance with this, no alter was
higher than the home altar, which had a mystical presence.
Like the Bible, it could heal those who come to it for succor.
Many young men have been saved from temptation by women who
availed themselves of the spiritual effect of a cozy home.
The home was woman's shrine, throne and empire, "more holy
that cloister, more saintly and pure than church or altar."[43]
In short, the wife was the household goddess.

HBS believed that the love of woman was a saving force,
that women were special instruments of God's grace; their
physical beauty was an inspiration and their love had redeeming powers for they were finer, more tender and devoted, and
less open to temptation than men. She suggested to Lady
Byron that in the afterlife she would see Byron purified and
would know that "to you it has been given, by your life of
love and faith, to accomplish this glorious change."[44] Love
was a sacrament and women were best able to love, therefore,

"In matters of grace God sets a special value on woman's
nature and design to put special honor upon it" and the
clergy should enumerate woman's influence among the means of
grace. [45]

THE VICTORIAN WOMAN ON A PEDESTAL

Stowe did not stand alone in advocating the "gospel of
womanhood." She was typical of her time, one of the many
advocates of women's saving abilities. In a world no longer
sure of its beliefs, the adoration of Victorian women replaced the worship of saints. [46] Anxiety is a key word for
the Mid-Victorian world in all its flux and ferment. Americans turned to the security of the peaceful home and a
Protestant veneration of motherhood became a part of American
popular religion.

HBS offered her own explanation of the glorification of
womanhood. Women replaced the influence of aristocracy:
they are "something to be looked up to, petted, and court-
ed.... The American life would become vulgar and commonplace
did not a chivalrous devotion to women come in to supply the
place of recognized orders of nobility." [47]

Stowe's woman worship was typical of the Victorian era.
By the 1850's the nuclear family was well established as
child centered and mother directed. Its values, especially
romantic love and motherhood, were enforced by the central-
ized publishing industry, magazine serials, novels, poetry
and sermons. The fenced single frame dwelling materialized
its isolation. [48] *Godey's Ladies Magazine* summarized the
beliefs of woman worship: "Women's duties are of a much
higher and holier nature than man's inasmuch as to her is
consigned the moral power of the world." Or as a critic
Frances Wright viewed the Victorian creed, men "celebrate us
as angels and goddesses, and will not allow us to be flesh
and blood." [49]

Like Emerson, the Victorians saw woman as a civilizing
force "taming her savage mate, planting tenderness, hope and
eloquence in all whom she approaches."[50] "Angelic" was the
term most frequently used to describe women; in sermons,
novels and magazine stories women were said to speak with
"angel whisperings." To a young character in a magazine
story his beloved was like "a divinity," and his mother's
face emanated "holy, contemplative emotions which light up
her face as with the divinity of an angel...."[51] This coin
had another side, of course, which was not so beatific, for
while women were taught to think of themselves as a special
class, they were placed on pedestals and rarely allowed to
step down from them. Their world became a prison whose
dimensions were defined by the four walls of their homes or
churches. Women were viewed as temptresses as well as angels,
and were taught to be submissive to men, perhaps a manifestation of male hostility.[52] It was thus a double-edged sword
that was thrust at the Victorian woman: reverence on the one
hand and restriction on the other.

The highest ideal of womanhood was realized in the role
of the mother for upon the mother depended both nation and
race.[53] The husband was told to proudly bow his manly soul
in earnest worship before his wife, "for within that sacred
temple, so beautiful and consecrated to you, are concealed
the purity, the peace, the dignity, the glory, the very angel
guardian of your home."[54] Men could build ships and rail-
roads but not new members of the nation; though powerful as
queen, Victoria was much more powerful as the reigning emblem
of the empire of Motherhood.

In *The Empire of Mother* (1870) Henry Wright maintained
that the body and soul of the infant are dependent on the
condition of the mother during her pregnancy: as God's "high
priest" she stands "between God and her unborn babe."[55] It

is she who determines the destiny of her child. The mother
thus has the potential to be the Messiah and Savior of the
race. Wright preached the Gospel of Generation, he said, for
if mothers were well trained, there would be no need for
regeneration, as their "tender love and anxious sleepless
solicitude" would insure the spiritual and physical well-
being of the child.

Nor was Wright's an isolated view. The feminist Margaret
Fuller rhapsodized that "Earth knows no fairer, holier relation than that of mother...."[56] Bushnell attributed to
mothers powers of intuition and sentiment, in what has been
called the beginning of the feminine mystique.[57] In a poem a
Reverend Cheever proclaimed, "O 'tis a sacred, sweet and
fearful duty to train these earth-born spirits for the
skies."[58] To be wife and mother was holy, a source of grace
and power; the warrior hero in a poem, for example, needed no
helmet because his mother had kissed his golden hair and "she
guards me with a prayer."[59] Godey's magazine taught that
woman's duties are more holy than men's because to her is
assigned "the moral power of the world."[60] Thus women civil-
ized and Christianized not only their children but also their
husbands. By her presence and her example she aided in
"forming and improving the general manners, disposition and
conduct of the other sex...."[61]

Glorification of motherhood was a major theme of women
writers and is a natural outgrowth of the belief in women's
superior intuitive access to the higher realms, in contrast
to animalistic male aggression in the mundane world. As the
Reverend Antoinette Blackwell explained, feminine perception,
insight, and unselfishness evolved from her maternal biolog-
ical role. That the appeal of the virtues of motherhood was
powerful is evidenced by its use by radical feminists;
Elizabeth Cady Stanton, for example, used maternity as a
dominant theme in her editorship of the Women's Bible

published in the 1890's. Believing that the Bible was used
to degrade women, Stanton's committee looked for grounds on
which to reply to the Eve-as-temptress syndrome. They
turned to the Virgin Mary and her role as mother, glorifying
maternity and the virtues they saw arising from it, namely
love, intuition, refinement and the ability to inspire.
They also reinterpreted Eve's significance seeing her as
"more than man" due to her initiation of the quest for
knowledge, while Adam was passive.

They believed that woman's motherly piety would bring
redemption from "the darkness of the sensuous nature" represented by the male principle, for her "enlightened motherhood" radiated a civilizing influence, a force for peace and
the arts instead of the war and burnt offerings produced by
men.[62] As mothers of the race, they concluded, women have
been "the great factor in the building of the race; are they
not more sacred than churches, altars, sacraments or the
priesthood?"[63] The writers suggested that prayers should be
offered to a Heavenly Mother as well as to a Father.
Stanton postulated the glories of the ancient matriarchy
which was unfortunately destroyed by men; as opposed to the
positive female influence, the male influence is destructive
and selfish. She deduced that "women might in fact be
superior in that their maternal instincts were the source of
civilization.

Another example of a radical ensnared in the glorification of motherhood was Victoria Woodhull: spiritualist
society president, candidate for the United States presidency,
stockbroker, speaker on women's rights, and editor of a
weekly newspaper. Later in her life, Woodhull received a
vision from Jesus Christ to exalt motherhood. Her sister,
Tennie C. Claflin (sic: a name she cleverly selected for
herself), looked for a millenium headed by a matriarchy.
Stowe's half-sister Isabella Hooker dreamed of being the

matriarch. Claflin preached that women possess a "healthful,
saving, purifying power" that was needed to save the nation.[64]

The dangers of "matriology" were apparent to a few. One
who later realized the perils of overemphasis was feminist
Charlotte Perkins Gilman, HBS' great niece, who nevertheless
affirmed that female functions are "far more akin to human
functions," more atuned to life and love, and opposed to the
masculine emphasis on death and punishment in religion.[65]
It is a short step from maternal virtue to moral superiority,
and it was a step the feminists easily made. The consensus
among both men and women, as stated by the framers of the
Seneca Falls Declaration of Women's Rights (1848), was that
"man, while claiming for himself intellectual superiority,
does accord to woman moral superiority..." and the women
adopted this belief in their attempt to find self-worth.

Mary Baker Eddy, founder of Christian Science, explained
that woman was "a higher idea of God than man" because Eve
was created later than Adam.[66] From physical evidence such
as the facts that woman's breasts were more developed and
she had less body hair and from psychological evidence--
woman was more peace-loving and pious, had a great love of
beauty--the reformer Eliza Farnham deduced that woman was
the more evolved sex. The male represents the more base
forces of energy and power, explained the feminist author
Margaret Fuller, while the female is associated with the
higher qualities of harmony and beauty.

Both men and women agreed that the influence of woman's
greater refinement was needed to civilize male politics and
government. She is the way to redemption, the new Adam,
preached Margaret Fuller, because she is more cultured and
elevated than man with "stronger electrical and magnetic
elements, and more open to the spiritual influx."[67] Antoinette Blackwell, the first ordained Congregational minister,

also taught that women were more cultivated and selfless and
that there is a direct correlation between the advancement
of a civilization and the degree of participation of women
in all spheres of life.

A corollary of the belief in woman's superiority was
the disparagement of males, especially the clergy, for their
misogynistic emphasis on woman's role as tempter and subordinate to her husband.   Blackwell complained that the male
clergy used any technique to keep women out of power,
including ridicule and 'scurrilous attacks."[68]   The Quaker
preacher Lucretia Mott charged that the pulpit had been
prostituted, the Bible ill-used, and that priestcraft had
subjugated women.   Stanton especially blamed Protestant
clergy for purging the feminine element from religion and
for subordinating women to men: she believed their priestcraft to be the major cause of women's oppression.   Ministers,
according to Sarah Grimké, used their position to organize a
"system of spiritual power and ecclesiastical authority,
which is now vested solely in the hands of men."[69]   Men were
seen as savages who needed women's refinement; Julia Ward
Howe, for example, located civilization's origins in woman's
lifting man out of "his natural savagery to share with her
the love of off-spring, the enjoyment of true and loyal
companionship."[70]

Reasons for woman worship were many; they included the
needs of the rising middle class and the desire for security
in an age of great flux.   This rising middle class wished to
distinguish itself from the lower classes by its manner,
etiquette, dress, speech and taboo words.   Woman bore the
brunt of the display of class consciousness and distinctive-
ness: her church attendance and piety "sheds respectability
on us," remarks Stowe's character St. Clare (*UTC*).[71]   As
imported from Europe, the idea of the fashionable lady

placed emphasis on clothes and the decorativeness of women
rather than on their intellectual attainments: the latter
could not be paraded as a measure of the material success of
the husband. According to John Quincy Adams, returning to
America from France at the end of the eighteenth century,
American women had become "affected" and "simpering" concerned solely with dancing and fashion.[72]

The burden of maintaining societal taboos often fell to
women: the middle class desire to be genteel and respectable reached an extreme in women who refused to say "leg"
and shunned even the term "limb." An English visitor,
Frances Trollope, reported that a group of women insisted
that lace be painted to cover up piano legs revealed on a
painted sign. Pregnancy was not a topic of polite conversa-
tion and newspapers did not publish birth notices. Mothers
of pupils at Troy Seminary for females in the 1830's were
shocked that their daughters were drawing diagrams of the
human heart and women would tell their doctors they had a
pain in the stomach when it was really in an unmentionable
breast. Prudery transcended its middle class origins and
became dominant in the Victorian world.

In addition to being socio-cultural signifiers, or as
HBS stated, "the custom-makers of society," genteel women
served as security which was greatly needed in an age of
major changes. Marxism, Darwinism, historical criticism of
the Bible, doubt about traditional religious values, proliferation of sects, the rapid growth of cities, technological
advances, and immigration, labor strikes, the pressures of
work and competition in an age of booms and panics and
depressions--all these caused anxiety. A stepped-up living
pace contributed to the nervousness of the age. Speed was
the new motif: railroad speed went from twelve to fifty
miles per hour in a few years, and steamboats left sailing

vessels in their wake. There was a prevailing sense of
being driven. Economically there were more goods being
produced, and hence more pressure to work harder to buy
them. In this hectic world of vast and often heedless
change, Social Darwinism provided the ideological scenario
for life experienced as a struggle for survival.

It was in this milieu that the family assumed a new
importance as a haven of calm in the alienation, rush and
competition of industrial society and its chief product--the
city. The family prayed together, read aloud in the eve-
nings, had its annual vacation and its photograph album. At
home, explained Thomas Carlye, "we cease the struggle in the
race of the world, and give our hearts leave and leisure to
love."[73] The family had to be preserved at all costs against
the onslaught of radical politics, atheism, Marxism, the
breaking apart of the Puritan synthesis, and growing sexual
license. The family replaced the older institutions of
court and church as symbol for stability, order and moral
purpose.

Still another explanation is that "Woman-the-mother is
the golden ideal, the convenient repository for man's most
unexamined, unwanted, sentimentalized, suffocating, ahuman
notions about his own composite being."[74] That is, she is
the recipient of male projections, for qualities which are
not useful to him in achieving worldly success. As idealized priestess of the home, woman was stripped of human
sexual passion and supposed to submit passively to the male
passion of her spouse. She was so important for security
that she had to be rendered controllable and predictable.
There could never be an American Venus, nor would an American
Virgin ever dare command, wrote Henry Adams in his *Autobiography*, for American art, language and education were "as
far as possible sexless. Society regarded this victory over
sex as its greatest triumph...."[75]

The nineteenth century's denial of woman's sexuality
can be linked with capitalism's need for orderly, predictable behavior, while the colonial era had a healthy realistic
attitude toward both male and female sexuality. Passions
were unpredictable and thus undesirable--therefore in the
woman the play of the passions had to be restricted to the
family structure, if not completely eradicated. Female
passions were negated as a threat to the status quo.[76]

The rebels--such as Victoria Woodhull and Tennie C.
Claflin, John Humphrey Noyes, and Utopian socialist Robert
Dale Owen, who advocated birth control to relieve women from
sexual slavery--were considered fearful iconoclasts. The
reaction to increased sexual freedom--without the protection
of a closely knit community such as the Puritans had--
resulted in a denial of sex to women, except in the context
of marriage, where it was seen to be a duty rather than the
spontaneous fulfillment of passion.[77] Religious fervor was
an outlet for sexual expression. Passion was directed
away from earthy men to Christ as the ideal love figure.
HBS was certainly an example of a woman passionately devoted
to her betrothed Jesus.

In rejecting the theology of her childhood, HBS substi-
tuted the Romantic emphasis on love and the feelings of the
heart, instead of intellectual systems of theology. She
identified men with intellect and women with heart as did
many other nineteenth century thinkers. Black men were also
seen in the same mode as women, creatures of simple faith in
Christ. She found women and womanlike men such as Uncle
Tom to be most like Jesus in their self-sacrifice, humility
and love. She thus looked to women rather than to male
clergy caught up in dogmatic disputations to save souls.
She was a major popularizer of the Victorian adoration of
the woman on the pedestal kept distant from actual participation in life outside the home. She helped to define a

cult of woman worship by asserting that it was imperative
that woman be a loving mother and/or wife in order to save
her family. Such Romantic writers as Scott, Byron, and
Carlyle provided her with a philosophy with which to frame
her rebellion against the male clergy and her substitution
of women as the primary examples of righteousness.

NOTES

[1] HBS, *Poganuc People*, p. 179.

[2] HBS, *Religious Sketches*, p. 210.

[3] HBS, *Dred*, Vol. 1, p. 363.

[4] HBS, *Religious Sketches*, p. 206.

[5] HBS, *My Wife and I*, p. 28.

[6] HBS, *Old Town Folks*, V. 2, p. 8.

[7] HBS, *Dred*, V. 1., p. 438.

[8] HBS, *Agnes of Sorrento*, p. 153.

[9] Fields, *Life and Letters of Harriet Beecher Stowe*, pp. 256 and 207.

[10] HBS, *Dred*, V. 2, p. 43. The other pole of the Good Mother feminine archetype (as described by Carl Jung and Erich Neumann) is the Terrible Mother who engulfs, destroys, enchants, bewitches, and tempts. Stowe did use such terms for unawakened women--Sally and Nina were called witches before their conversions. She described other women as viragos and tyrants, and as tempting daughters of Eve or Pandora. Like some twentieth century feminists, she was intrigued by the notion of androgyny; she wrote that Plato thought "the only perfect human thinker and philosopher who will ever arise will be the MAN-WOMAN, or a human being who unites perfectly the nature of the two sexes." (HBS, *Old Town Folks*, V. 2, p. 55.) (This is indeed where the individual self is headed, to form a hybrid of masculine and feminine archetypes, according to Jung and Neumann.)

[11] HBS, *Religious Sketches*, p. 232.

[12] HBS, *Old Town Folks*, V. 2, p. 235.

[13] HBS, *Poganuc People*, p. 218.

[14]Charles Stowe, *Harriet Beecher Stowe*, p. 477.

[15]HBS, *We and Our Neighbors*, p. 161.

[16]HBS, *Old Town Folks*, V. 2, p. 55.

[17]Another factor in her distrust of theology was its
use by ministers to defend slavery. She believed that they
avoided the voice of conscience by discussing doctrines.
They harmed the anti-slavery cause. They also harmed the
cause of women by teaching that the only avenue open to a
girl of "good family" was marriage. Her criticism of ministers was illustrated in her Dr. Cushing, who was "opposed to
anything which made trouble" (HBS, *We and Our Neighbors*,
p. 107).

[18]HBS, *Dred*, V. 1, p. 276.

[19]Crozier, *The Novels of Harriet Beecher Stowe*, p. 167.

[20]HBS, *Old Town Folks*, V. 2, p. 85.

[21]HBS, *Stories, Sketches*, p. 76.

[22]HBS, *The Minister's Wooing*, p. 280.

[23]HBS to Annie Fields, 30 November, 1881, Box 58, Huntington Archives, San Marino, California.

[24]HBS, *Religious Sketches*, p. 232.

[25]HBS, *Uncle Tom's Cabin*, pp. 243-44. HBS, *My Wife and
I*, pp. 243-44.

[26]In *Minister's Wooing* Mary was a good fairy, a saint,
a living gospel, who had "strange power" to inspire boys.
She was a "pure priestess of a domestic temple" (p. 230).
Other women were also outstanding: her mother was an object
of awe and wonder to her husband; Mrs. Marvyn was more sensitive and intelligent than her spouse, and Candace patronized
her mate and was a kind of preacher. In *Pearl of Orr's
Island* Mara was described as a good fairy, a fairy princess,
an angel, a saint whose touch brought peace and whose pious
death brought salvation to Moses and Sally. In addition,

spinster healer Miss Roxy was a "sort of priestess and sibyl"
(p. 19). In *Agnes of Sorrento* Agnes was a divinity to
Agostino and an inspiration to her confessor. In *Old Town
Folks* Tina had the ability to inspire men with a magnetic
power to "excite the higher faculty." She was "one of the
species of womankind that used to be sought out as priest-
esses to the Delphic oracle." Old Madame Kittery inspired
devotion, and Harry's mother was saintly--"no theology had
the power of her last counsel." In *Pink and White Tyranny*
Grace's influence inspired her lover and her brother. Lillie's
daughter was "sacred and saintly." Lillie's husband was a
"romantic adorer of womanhood, as a sort of divine mystery,
--a never ending poem" (*PWT*, p. 296).

Other examples of pious women found in male literature are
Dickens' Little Nell in *The Old Curiosity Shop*, Rose and
Nancy in *Oliver Twist*, and Lizzie in *Our Mutual Friend*.
Sir Walter Scott added to the Victorian cult of womanhood
both through his novels and his criticism of other novels
from 1810-1830. In Carlyle's *Sartor Resartus*, Teufelsdrockh
viewed nature as a benevolent Mother, but was led to his
insights through the suffering caused by rejection by his
angel sweetheart, Blumine, who left him for a richer man.

It is difficult to find examples of female savior figures in
nineteenth century American male authored novels except for
the common theme of women as civilizers (Tom's aunt, and
Becky in Twain's *Tom Sawyer*, the wives of whalers in
Melville's *Moby Dick*). There is a paucity of strong female
heroines. Hawthorne perhaps comes closest: he suggests that
the spokesperson of a coming revelation will be a woman, but
a pure one. Hester's daughter Pearl offers no hope of reform
of male/female relationships but safely marries in Europe and
conforms to societal norms, although not Puritan ones. The
men in *The Blithedale Romance* fall in love with childlike
but pure Priscilla rather than passionate, proud, intelligent
feminist Zenobia (who is based on Margaret Fuller). In
Howells' *The Rise of Silas Lapham* his wife is the conscience,
but in the end he is more moral than she. Sister Soulsby
teaches the hero of *The Damnation of Theron Ware* (by Harold
Frederic) to function again in society, but her reputation
is tarnished by her earlier activities. Henry James' heroines seek for independence and meet death or martyrdom as a
result: Daisy Miller incurred fatal malaria on an expedition
to the Colliseum; his Maggie in *The Golden Bowl* endures her
husband's extra-marital affair, until the end of the novel;
Verena in *The Bostonians* gives up her involvement in the
woman's movement to marry a man whose ideas she strongly dis-
agrees with; his Isabel in *The Portrait of a Lady* wants
independence but enters into a marriage she regrets but main-
tains in order to care for her husband's daughter. In being

so unselfish she is a kind of savior figure. Women writers
kill off their strong heroines just as males do; for example,
Kate Chopin's character Edna's search for independence from
her husband and children ends in suicide in *The Awakening*.
Thus, women were portrayed favorably by men as pious and
pure when they stayed within the confines of domesticity and
subordination to husband and children. When they sought
independence, death or martyrdom was the result. HBS also
safely located her saviors in the home; but she, like other
women writers, goes further than men in making women soul
savers in addition to being civilizers and refiners of taste
and morality.

[27]Sklar, *Catharine Beecher*, p. XIV. HBS used her sister's
concept and terminology as when she urged her twins to rise
to "generous self-sacrifice," and told them her idea of God
was a being who had "no self--who lives only in loving and
giving." (12 or 31 May 1859, Folder 103, Brooklyn, 20 March
1859, Folder 103, Schlesinger Archives.)

[28]Catharine Beecher, *Common Sense Applied to Religion*,
p. 257.

[29]Letter 30 June 1845 as quoted by Wilson, *Patriotic
Gore*, p. 22.

[30]For example, the influence of one of her characters
over her minister husband was described as "like that of the
soul over the body." (HBS, *My Wife and I*, p. 33.)

[31]HBS, *My Wife and I*, p. 72; *The Minister's Wooing*,
p. 131.

[32]Letter 29 July 1845, as quoted by Wilson, *Patriotic
Gore*, p. 24.

[33]HBS, *Old Town Folks*, V. 1, p. 368.

[34]HBS, *Stories, Sketches*, p. 65.

[35]HBS, *Religious Sketches*, p. 37.

[36]Crozier contends with this, maintaining that Stowe's
model was Sarah Edwards (Crozier, *The Novels of Harriet
Beecher Stowe*, p. 133), and the other young women included
in Edwards' *Personal Narrative*.

[37]HBS, *Sunny Memories of Foreign Lands*, (Boston:
Phillips, Sampson & Co., 1854), V. 1, p. 256.

[38]HBS, *My Wife and I*, pp. 97-98.

[39]Mary Ryan further develops this point, noting that
female novelists often did away with a male hero, revealing
a "latent animosity." Mary Ryan "American Society and The
Cult of Domesticity, 1830-1860," (Ph.D. Dissertation, University of California at Santa Barbara, 1971), p. 281.

[40]HBS, *My Wife and I*, p. 195.

[41]HBS, *House and Home Papers*, p. 48.

[42]According to Crozier (*The Novels of Harriet Beecher
Stowe*, p. 166) this concern for aesthetics replaced her
evangelicalism after the Civil War.

[43]HBS, *The Minister's Wooing*, p. 566.

[44]HBS, *Lady Byron Vindicated*, (New York: Haskell House,
1970, first published 1870), p. 400.

[45]HBS, *Dred*, V. 1, p. 357.

[46]Female chastity was a means for repression of the
pleasure principle which Freud viewed as a requisite of civilization. Francoise Basch, *Relative Creatures: Victorian
Women in Society*, (New York: Shocken, 1970), p. 271.

[47]HBS, *My Wife and I*, p. 396.

[48]Alternatives to the nuclear family were attempted but
were feared and opposed. Mother Ann Lee's celibate Shaker
communities separated men and women (formally organized in
New York in 1787). John Humphrey Noyes' Oneida experiment
with complex marriage began in the 1840s; he was opposed to
"special love" between a couple as selfish and unChristian,
as there was no marriage in heaven and marriage was slavery
for women. Instead everyone in the community was married to
each person and practiced planned parenthood. Women cut
their hair, shortened their skirts and learned the same skills
as men. Mormon Joseph Smith also increased the sexual avail-
ability of women to men in his revelation of plural marriage.

In so doing he "made of sexuality a means to celestial glory"
(Thomas O'Dea, *The Mormons*, Chicago: The University of
Chicago Press, 1957, p. 60).

[49]Robert Riegel, *American Women: A Story of Social
Change* (Rutherford: Fairleigh Dickinson Univ. Press, 1971),
pp. 215 and 225.

[50]Perry Miller, *The American Transcendentalists*, (New
York: Doubleday Anchor Books, 1957), p. 181.

[51]"Cottage Life," *Graham's*, V. XIX, No. 1 (July, 1841),
p. 2.

[52]Martha Vicinus, *Suffer and Be Still: Women in the
Victorian Age*, (Bloomington: Indiana Univ. Press, 1973),
p. 167.

[53]In the 1600s Baxter put a special responsibility on
mothers to bring their children to Christ, for their affections were tender and they spent more time with their children than did fathers (Baxter, *Saints Everlasting Rest*,
p. 149).

[54]Henry Wright, *The Empire of Mother* (Boston: W. White,
1870), p. 77.

[55]Ibid., p. 110.

[56]Margaret Fuller, *Women in the Nineteenth Century*
(Boston: Roberts Brothers, 1895), p. 96.

[57]Sklar, *Catharine Beecher*, p. 162.

[58]*Graham's Magazine*, V. XXI, No. 1 (July 1842), p. 44.

[59]*Putnam's Magazine*, V. 5, No. XXXI, (October, 1857),
p. 395.

[60]Robert Riegel, *American Women: A STory of Social
Change*, (Rutherford: Fairleigh Dickinson Univ. Press, 1970),
p. 225.

[61]Charles Butler, *The American Lady*, (Philadelphia:
Hogan and Thompson, 1830), p. 15.

[62]Elizabeth Stanton, et al., *Woman's Bible*, (New York: European Publishing Co., 1895), V. 2, p. 186.

[63]Ibid., V. 1, p. 76.

[64]Page Smith, *Daughters of the Promised Land*, (Boston: Little, Brown, 1970), p. 148.

[65]Jean Friedman and William Shade, eds., *Our American Sisters*, (Boston: Allyn and Bacon, 1973), p. 207. Gilman's theory seems to be borne out by women founders of sects and denominations. Mary Baker Eddy, for example, taught that evil had no reality and that the idea of a fallen state of being is an illusion. Antoinette Blackwell left her position as a Congregationalist minister because she could not accept belief in eternal punishment for innate depravity. Of course, this was not a view monopolized by women; Emerson and his followers are male examples.

[66]Georgine Milmine, *The Life of Mary Baker Eddy and The History of Christian Science*, (New York: Doubleday, Page & Co., 1909), p. 188.

[67]Margaret Fuller, *Women in the Nineteenth Century*, p. 102.

[68]Mrs. Claude Gilson, unpublished biography of Antoinette Blackwell, Schlesinger ARchives, p. 72.

[69]Sarah Grimké, *Letters on the Equality of the Sexes*, (New York: Ben Franklin, 1910), p. 119.

[70]William O'Neil, *Everyone Was Brave: The Rise and Fall of American Feminism*, (Chicago: Quadrangle Books, 1969), p. 36.

[71]HBS, *Uncle Tom's Cabin*, p. 199. Thorsten Veblen noted the use of women as objects of conspicuous consumption, by their idleness, tokens that their husbands were financially successful. He compared hoop skirts with Chinese foot binding, as both made women nonproductive. Moral zeal also served as a substitute for religious certainty and was rooted in Wesleyan evangelical revival according to Gertrude Himmelfarb, *Victorian Minds*, (New York: Alfred A. Knopf, 1968), pp. 278, 303.

[72]Smith, *Daughters of the Promised Land*, p. 59.

[73]Houghton, *The Victorian Frame of Mind*, (New Haven: Yale Univ. Press, 1957), p. 45.

[74]Vivian Gornick and Barbara Moran, eds., *Women in Sexist Society*, (New York: Signet, 1971), p. 138.

[75]Henry Adams, *The Education of Henry Adams*, (New York: Modern Library, 1931), p. 385.

[76]The U. S. Congress passed a law against shipping birth control devices or information through the mails, in the Comstock Act of 1873. The increase of prostitution and illegitimate births was also a threat to the sanctity of marriage bonds. There were around 20,000 prostitutes in New York in the 1860s (Smith, *Daughters of the Promised Land*, p. 228), and an estimated 8,000 illegitimate births out of 36,000 births in New York in 1870 (Riegel, *American Women*, p. 92).

[77]From Paul to Augustine to Chaucer, women were reminded of the debt of their bodies to their husbands. In the *Parson's Tale*, Chaucer remarks, "She hath merite of chastitee that yieldeth to hire housbonde the dette of hir body, ye, though it be agayn hir likynge and the hiest of hire herte." But he noted that sexuality only for amorous love was a "deedly synne." (F. N. Robinson, ed., *The Poetical Works of Chaucer*, Boston: Houghton Mifflin Co., 1933, p. 308.)

CHAPTER FOUR

SALVATION COMPREHENDED IN ROMANTIC CONTEXT

ROMANTIC EVANGELICALISM

While Harriet Beecher Stowe and Henry Ward Beecher
shared a Romantic theology, Henry looked to Nature as the
medium for God's revelation and conversion and Harriet
looked to the family. They were key spokespersons for the
revolution in theology from Calvinism to Liberal Protestantism in the Mid-Victorian era of 1840-70. Love was the key
emotion for both and both craved it in their own lives:
Henry complained that Lyman was too busy to be loved, while
their stepmother Harriet was too distant--"I like above all
things in the world to be loved," he revealed at age twenty-
seven. And as a teenager Harriet saw that "This desire to
be loved forms, I fear, the great motive for all my actions."[1]

They found their main source of love in Christ, their
Friend and Brother. They considered their mother's devotion
to them the highest form of earthly love. In Henry's novel
Norwood a character describes his mother as having "the
sense of infiniteness; a mysteriousness more than any I have
ever known."[2] Henry, who revered women in general, believed
that they were like angels and that their purpose was the
refinement of mankind.[3]

Like true Romantics they shared their eldest sister's
dislike for their father's theological disputation. Henry
said that he himself preached no doctrines, "only Christ,"
and through a character in his novel he averred his weariness
with "logic and argument and doctrine and discussion."[4]
Harriet and Henry shared other Romantic tenets as well:
most prominent among them was a fascination with the past
and with nature.

Dionysian emotion, sensation, intuition, the supernatural, imagination, and fantasy were believed by Romantics

to be more valid than reason, logic and intellect. Romantics were concerned with what they called "the heart." If
one uses Freudian terminology, Romantics were concerned with
libido rather than superego.

Leslie Fiedler saw the Romanticism of the late eighteenth to the middle nineteenth centuries as the break-
through of the ancient mother goddess mythology which had
resurfaced earlier in the cult of courtly love during the
eleventh century, then in the cult of the Virgin, and was to
manifest itself again in sentimental novels, beginning with
Samuel Richardon's, in the mid-eighteenth century. The
return of the goddess meant, "not only few forays into
inwardness but a denial of reigning ideologies and dogmas."[5]
The mother goddess continued to assert herself against the
repression of male dominated hierarchies of church and
culture. Women like Madame de Staël were prominent as
Romantic authors or in writing forerunners to the Romantic
novel, such as Ann Radcliffe's eighteenth century Gothic
novels of terror.[6]

Harriet and Henry were part of the evangelical movement
of the first half of the nineteenth century. This movement
acknowledged the importance of the emotions and, in so
doing, helped the evangelicals carry Romanticism into religious life.

The Romantic connection of the passion of love with the
supernatural influenced the evangelical movement in America
just as evangelicalism with its emotional conversion experience was a strength to English Romanticism in the early
nineteenth century. Evangelicalism in America was shaped by
Romanticism after 1835. It was the nexus for Stowe's intellectual development. McLoughlin defined the impact of
Romantics on this stage of evangelicalism as: (1) emphasis
on the heart; (2) a Christocentric emphasis on the personality of Jesus; and (3) idealization of women, children, and

parenthood as the "most perfect embodiment if not the most
efficient means of grace."[7] These three characteristics of
Romantic evangelicalism are hallmarks of Stowe's gospel. It
was sentimentalized by popular preachers and lecturers such
as Horace Bushnell, Henry Ward Beecher, and Ralph Waldo
Emerson.

Key words to describe the Romantic evangelical style
are: intuition, imagination, heart, feeling, subjectivity,
anti-rationalism, concern for process and history, and above
all, love. In the pantheon of virtues, love had a higher
place than doctrinal knowledge; subsequently there were
anti-intellectual overtones: angels and devils arrive
intellectually at the same place, explained evangelist
Charles Finney, but they are distinguished by the makeup of
the heart. Finney set the precedent for no popular evangelist to attend a major university or seminary. Evangelicals
made heart and home the key to salvation. Home became the
model of heaven and the mother the archetype of the self-
sacrificing Christ. The theory that "mystical and perfec-
tionist religion," as seen in Romantic evangelicalism,
thrives when feminine influence is dominant may be given some
credence.[8]

The doctrines of Romantic evangelicalism are reflected
in Stowe's novels. Scorning reliance on logic we must, she
wrote, "trust the influence of our hearts above reason."[9]
Love was her savior, as personified in Jesus. He was the
Friend whose love, like the sunlight, could cast aside the
clouds of theological speculation. On earth, love was manifested in the family, where the woman's work was to perform
her ministry, making those around her "feel the sole worth
and value of love." Love induced salvation or, in HBS'
terminology, the coming in or awakening of a soul.[10] The
gospel of love was best preached by example, specifically
that of the relationship of close friends and relatives who

had childlike access to the simple gospel preached in the
Sermon on the Mount. It was, HBS pointed out, the children
in the temple who received Jesus as messiah, while the chief
priests and scribes scowled. Those souls were saved that
had closest contact with the heart.

HBS' USE OF ROMANTICISM

Romantic writers such as Byron, Scott, Burns, Madame de
Staël, and Goethe all had an impact on HBS' philosophy and
style. It is important therefore to isolate the components
of Romanticism and examine what Stowe accepted or rejected
of its philosophy.

First, Stowe's own use of the term designated the
unusual and the mysterious; for example, "The young folks
called the rocks and glens and rivers of their romantic
region by names borrowed from Scott and Byron."[11] Or, she
wrote to Calvin of Venice, "It is all romance from beginning
to end, and never ceases to seem strange and picturesque."[12]

Like Romantic writers such as Scott, she was concerned
with a romanticized history of a particular people--for her,
the Puritans of New England. She was fascinated by the
American equivalent of the savage, the blacks, and she was a
pioneer in exploring dialect and local color. She also
delighted in contrasts and oppositions, like those between
Uncle Tom and Eva, Topsy and Eva, Mrs. St. Claire and Miss
Ophelia, and Mr. St. Claire and his twin brother.

She was also devoted to nature. Stowe combined both a
Romantic veneration of nature and an Edwardsian view of
nature, seeing it as brutal and dangerous. Her hero Dred is
a good example of the former. A black renegade, he lives in
the wilderness of the swamp, quoting the Old Testament like
the prophet he is. Stowe explained that, "So completely had
he come into sympathy and communion with nature" that he
experienced "visions and communications" and "predictions
and intimations."[13]

Her heroines join in the Romantic flower worship and
bedeck themselves with flowers. They love to walk in the
woods where HBS believed their taste was refined as Stowe
was herself by the "sweet thoughts" that came to her in her
garden work. Like Byron, she referred to nature as a good
Mother. She also placed it above books and intellect as a
teacher; in a poem she told her readers that in the Spring
one should put books aside and "dance with the seeded grass
in fringy play...and float with Nature all the livelong
day."[14]

Yet Stowe also kept her Puritan regard for the uncon-
trolled majesty and terror of nature. She recognized the
earlier notion of nature, as taught in her childhood, as the
tempter and antithesis of grace and sometimes viewed it as
alien, feeling herself "tossed a whirling sensitive atom
among the uncontrollable unexplicable laws of maker and
time."[15] She had her character Bolton speak of the "grind-
ing and clashing of natural laws--laws of whose operation
they are ignorant and yet whose penalties are inexorable."[16]
She explained that nature destroys the weak and the maimed,
in contrast to the higher power, Christianity, which aims to
save even the one lost sheep.[17]

She also manifested the Romantic view of the validity
of what she called "heart consciousness" as contrasted with
the evil effects of intellect. She believed that love was
"the strongest of all powers," and a "happy divinity,"
defining Jesus as LOVE. She believed that women were more
spiritual, refined and elevated precisely because of their
openness to the loving promptings of the heart.

The supernatural and the occult fascinated her as it
did the Romantics. HBS believed in invisible spirits, some
of whom were protecting or guardian angels, and others
mischievous or malicious. She consulted mediums, used the
planchette or ouija board, was interested in phrenology,

talked of auras (not her term) around people, and at least
once used the language of astrology when she said, "This
particular Saturday afternoon all the constellations were
favorable." She believed that possibly the soul has "com-
pressed and unconscious powers" of spiritual insight and
divination.[18] She reported that she often had luminous
visions of scriptural passages in the time between sleeping
and waking. As a boy her husband Calvin had visions of
fairies, of a spirit child named Harvey, of a dark cloud
vortex. He continued to see visions in his adulthood,
including visions of Harriet.

THE ORIGINS OF HBS' ROMANTICISM

Stowe's involvement with Romanticism began with the
Byron fever which affected young people in Litchfield at the
time she was ten. Her father Lyman believed that Byron's
potential for greatness could have been saved for the Lord
if Nathaniel "Taylor and I might have got him out of his
troubles."[19] When Byron died, Lyman preached a stirring
sermon on the moral impact Byron could have made if he had
been a true Christian: afterward Harriet went to lie among
the daisies and think of Byron's fate in the afterlife. He
was the single greatest literary influence on her, then came
Sir Walter Scott and Dickens. Harriet discovered Byron's
poem *The Corsair* at her Aunt Esther's Litchfield home. She
read it voraciously, as she did any fiction she could find.
The Corsair centers around a typical Byronic hero, the
pirate Conrad. He is spirited, noble, haughty, passionate,
with "feeling fearful, and yet undefined." He was not at
peace with his world; the one living thing he did not hate
was his beloved Medora. She was his only hope on earth. He
gave to her loyally "Love, wild and strange."[20] But even
his one hope was extinguished: when he was captured, Medora
mistakenly believed him dead and committed suicide. When he

returned to his island hideaway and found her dead, he
immediately left the island forever, a lost soul.

Stowe scholars tract the influence of Conrad and other
passionate, despairing heroes in Stowe's novels: Ellery
Davenport (OTF), Aaron Burr (MW), Agostino Sarelli (Agnes),
Dred (Dred), and Simon Legree and St. Claire (UTC) have been
characterized as Byronic.   These characters, except for St.
Claire, Dred, and Agostino, who were restored to faith in
Christianity by women, are villains.   Byron was depicted as
a corrupt destroyer of morality in Stowe's attack on him in
Lady Byron Vindicated, published in 1870.[21]

However, HBS was fascinated with her villains, feeling
emotions she ascribed to them, namely "those periods of
distress when the heart secretly longs for what the mind has
rejected"--childhood religious beliefs.   Her Byronic male
characters felt a "relation to the universe as passionate
and as dangerous as anything the old [Puritan] creed demanded."[22] Davenport, for example, was often very philo-
sophical and searching; he recognized too that he was poison-
ed by the deterministic ultra-Calvinism of his youth.   He,
Stowe, and Byron had rebelled against the severe Presbyterian
Calvinism of their childhood, but retained its scars.

Byron's heroines also influenced Stowe's heroines: his
Aura Raby in Don Juan was ethereal, innocent and beautiful
as were Stowe's young women.   However, the other women in
Don Juan are not angelically innocent but are sensual.   The
native maiden Haidee, the Sultana, and the Russian empress
are all concerned with sexual pleasure.   Sexuality predomi-
nated in Byron's view of women.

Furthermore, Byron believed that love and marriage
rarely are found together.   His concern with sexuality was
certainly unlike Stowe's female characters who were without
sexual passion, a claim that she also made for herself.   She
did deal with men's sexuality but only from a negative

viewpoint as illicit and cruel; for example, in *Dred*,
alcoholic Tom Gordon wishes to seduce his half-brother's
wife and in *Uncle Tom's Cabin* Simon Legree attempts to
ravish Cassy and Evangeline.[23] Byron's influence on Stowe
is seen more in her male characters than in her female ones.

The works of two other Romantic writers, Scott and
Burns, were given to Harriet as a child by her Uncle George
Foote at Nutplains. He had the most profound influence on
her intellectual development, in the judgment of her son
Charles and grandson Lyman.[24] He was Catholic in his tastes,
broadened by his world travel as a sailor. Lyman Beecher
also read Scott's novels with his children, stopping to
discuss theological issues which he drew from the narrative.
Scott and Byron were the only novelists he allowed his
children to read, so they memorized long passages from Scott
and acted out his stories. Indeed, Harriet read *Ivanhoe*
seven times in one summer.

From Scott she learned the form of the historic novel
and his concern for a more interesting preindustrial past.
She was also influenced by his view that a novel should
contain a lesson and that it should be of moral value. His
interest in peasants was perhaps reflected in her interest
in blacks and their dialect.

Ivanhoe must have influenced her portrayal of women as
more moral and spiritual than men, with the ability to save
or doom them. The major women characters in *Ivanhoe*,
Rowena and Rebecca, have more character, depth and nobility
than the two major male characters. Ivanhoe was never very
visible as a personality, but was rather a type of the
knight. The templar was a false Christian, a brigand, and
attempted seducer and rapist of Rebecca.

Lady Rowena is described as noble, tall, pious and
lofty. Rebecca, the Jewess, is beautiful, skilled in medi-
cal arts, has strength of mind, and a strong and observing

character. She is generous, wise, and places her reliance
on heaven. As a result, her father frequently valued her
opinions above his own. She is described as an "angel from
heaven" with "a dignity that seemed more than mortal."[25]
She is true to her filial duties as when she does not allow
her unattainable love for Ivanhoe to overpower her obliga-
tions to her father.

Scott's women, like Stowe's, have the power to lead men
to evil as well as good. The Templar explained that "It was
woman that taught me cruelty" when he was rejected by an
unfaithful lover.[26] As a consequence, he was doomed to ill
fortune: "My manhood must know no domestic home, must be
soothed by no affectionate wife." Ulrica, an old Saxon
woman, was another who caused evil in the lives of men who
knew her, but they had first robbed her of her sexual virtue.
On the pedestal were Rebecca and Rowena who were the inspirational guiding lights bestowing piety and moral fortitude.
They could easily with only a change of costume step into
the New England kitchens of Stowe's Puritan women and continue as pious angels from heaven.

She was deeply moved by Madame de Staël's *Corinne*,
which asked, "Ought not every woman, like every man, to
follow the bent of her own talents?" She commented on
Corinne in a letter to her friend Georgianna May, "In
America feelings vehement and absorbing like hers become
still more deep, morbid, and impassioned by the constant
habits of self-government which the rigid forms of our
society demand."[27] Stowe knew herself to be a victim of
morbid feelings caused by worry over her salvation.

Another Romantic work that Stowe read was Goethe's
Faust and Calvin Stowe carried *Faust* around in his pocket.
Again the heroine, Gretchen, is innocent and natural and the
male, Faust, is closer to the demonic but was saved by
Margaret's deep sentiment.

Dickens, a Victorian more than a Romantic, was also
read by HBS. His Little Nell was a likely pattern for Eva.
Dickens was partly responsible for what has been called the
slaughter of the innocents in American novels. Despite his
own unhappy marriage, he also glorified the ideal of the
family kept together by the "good angel" of a woman. He,
too, believed in the power of the heart; his Gradgrind in
Hard Times was a negative symbol of cold reason. Yet
another theme of Dickens' that HBS duplicated was his concern that his novels serve a purpose to fight social ills.
He was concerned with poverty while Stowe focused on the
ills of slavery and urban life. Other English authors who
centered on the redeeming powers of woman's love included
Charlotte Brontë, Mrs. Gaskell, Thackeray, and George Eliot
with whom Stowe corresponded.

The books which most influenced her during her childhood are varied. In Litchfield, Harriet adored reading
Cotton Mather's tales of the past in his *Magnalia Christi
Americana*. She read it avidly, curled up in her father's
study intrigued by the romantic tales of witchcraft and the
"wonders of the Invisible World." She reported that reading
about the Puritans "made me feel the very ground I trod on
to be consecrated by some special dealing of God's providence."[28]

She also loved *Arabian Nights* and the fragment of *Don
Quixote* she found in an old box of books. Defoe's stories
and their travel plots influenced her. The English novelist
Samuel Richardson's character Sir Grandison was adopted by
Harriet's mother as her ideal man and Lyman read aloud from
Milton and Edwards. HBS also read *The Tempest*, but she
considered Shakespeare odd except for *The Tempest*, no doubt
redeemed because of the innocent character of Miranda, and
she thought Milton was "cold."

Nonfiction works supplied by Miss Pierce's Litchfield
Academy and by Harriet's Uncle Foote included: Paley's
Moral Philosophy, Blair's *Rhetoric*, Addison's *On Taste*,
and Bishop Herbert's *Life*. In Hartford, Butler's *Analogy of
Religion* and Baxter's *Saints Rest* were the two books that
made the greatest impression on her, especially the latter.
Her sister Catharine quoted Carlyle in letters written
during this time, so Harriet was probably exposed to his
ideas as well. She certainly knew of his concept of the
Hero who does the bidding of the moral law without thought
of his own pleasure.

During her trips to Europe, she met literary figures
such as Dickens, Elizabeth Browning, and Lady Byron. She
later corresponded with George Sand and George Eliot. She
also corresponded with American authors Longfellow, Whittier
and Holmes. She wrote articles about Hawthorne and Longfellow. Volumes of Longfellow, Whittier, Lowell, Holmes and
Hawthorne were selected by one of her characters as a wed-
ding gift and a character advocated reading Hawthorne,
Holmes and Emerson.

THE "SENTIMENTAL LOVE RELIGION"

Another major literary influence on Harriet Beecher
Stowe was the sentimental novel written in England and
America often by women for women. Novels were conduct books
for middle class women concerned with marriage and the
family. An era of sentimentality reigned in America from
around 1836 to 1860, although Richardson helped inaugurate
the form a century earlier. The sentimental novel differed
from the Romantic novel in that the former was produced by a
Victorian morality which severed reason and feeling. Sentimentality is "habitually to enjoy feelings without acting on
them."[29] It shared a Romantic emphasis upon sensibility and

feeling as the vehicles of truth, viewing women, blacks, and
primitives as the purest vessels of feeling. In the sentimental novel, feeling is all. Stowe was not quite a Victorian sentimentalist, for she was able to face--although
disdainfully--the reality of at least male sexual passion,
although it was always associated with wicked men, but she
was not an exuberant Romantic able to face passions between
men and women.

     Stowe was a spokeswoman of what Leslie Fiedler named
the "Sentimental Love Religion," where the "Pure Young Girl"
was the savior figure. The heroine brought her virginity to
bless marriage, the earthly equivalent of heavenly bliss.
She was the superego, civilizer and moral authority. The
male was the tempter, the evil seducer. When seduction
became too indecent for the Victorians, the male was portrayed as wicked, a drunken sot, lacking moral principle, or
he was ill or died in a moment of need, leaving the long
suffering woman with still more hardship to endure. Fiedler
speculated that American men accepted their emasculation by
women writers out of "self-punishment for desiring the women
postulated as living symbols of chastity and 'ethereal'
bliss."[30] He also suggested that America was bound to find
its security in women since it had defied its fathers:
fatherland, king, pope, and bishop. The hero in American
fiction was the "Good Bad Boy," like Tom Sawyer, who was
made to be reformed by the right women, first his mother,
then his wife.

     The architect of the "Sentimental Love Religion" was
Samuel Richardson, mid-eighteenth century author of *Pamela,*
Clarissa, and *Sir Charles Grandison.* Seduction of the
pure heroine was his motif. *Clarissa,* his best-seller, was
what Fiedler calls a bible of the "Sentimental Love Religion." Richardson's heroine was beset by a base aristocrat,
Lovelace, whom she loved but would not submit to his schemes

to take her virginity. He drugged her to rob her of her
maidenhead. He finally offered her marriage but she refused.
She spent many pages dying and then he was given his just
reward, killed in a duel with no prospect of going to
heaven.

Death was a common concern of the writers of sentimental
novels especially the death bed of young girls. HBS followed
the pattern of the killing of young girls such as Eva
(UTC), Nina (Dred) and Mara (Pearl). Her biographer Rourke
believed that Harriet Beecher Stowe was "half in love with
death," and Fiedler commented that, "not love but death is
Mrs. Stowe's true muse."[31] She did believe that the death
of a loved woman sometimes had more redeeming power than
life on earth.

What Richardson and Goldsmith had begun, women writers
reproduced prolifically. Middle class women were assigned
the domain of the home, while their men went out in the wide
world to work. Women used their leisure to read and write
novels. In the late eighteenth century they began to write
novels, not calling themselves authors but exemplary wives
and mothers. More than a third of the American novels
written before 1820 were by women. The high point for women
novelists was the era called the "feminine fifties" when
Hawthorne scorned the "d----d mob of scribbling women." It
began with a best-seller in 1850, The Wide Wide, World
by Susan and Anna Warner, followed by Uncle Tom's Cabin,
which was published in book form two years later.

A common theme in female fiction was the splendors of
marriage and motherhood. Marriage is "the most sacred tie
on earth," wrote Miss Southworth. Susan Warner wrote that,
"One woman will learn more wisdom from the child on her
breast than another will learn from ten thousand volumes."[32]
Of course every novel of Stowe's revolved around the spiritual powers of woman, as wife and mother.[33]

Yet another theme of the literary cult of womanhood was
the plantation legend that developed in Romantic contrast to
northern industrialism. The plantation was portrayed as a
kind of matriarchy with effete, indolent white men and women
possessed of strong moral character. Stowe utilized this
mythology in both her Southern novels.[34] For example, the
weak character of Little Eva's father is contrasted with her
piety, or the wicked Simon Legree is contrasted with the
virtuous Uncle Tom.

Perhaps the best male American author with which to com-
pare Stowe is Hawthorne, especially his heroines Hester in
The Scarlet Letter (1850), Phoebe in *The House of the Seven
Gables* (1851), and Hilda in *The Marble Faun* (1860). His
heroines also have a transformative impact on the heroes
but in the standard vein of woman as civilizer with much less
development of Stowe's theme of woman as main earthly channel
of grace. His heroines resemble HBS', especially Phoebe and
Hilda who are devout, simple, childlike, pure and lovely.
Hilda was described as a flower, an angel, fairy-like. Her
influence on Kenyon brought them back to the fold, to New
England, away from foreign Catholic Rome. Further, she
chastised him about his heresy of speculating that sin was
necessary for awareness of the moral life and depth of character. Her destiny was to be "enshrined and worshipped as
a household saint, in the light of her husband's fireside."
Kenyon looked to her as "my guide, my counselor, my inmost
friend, with that white wisdom which clothes you as a celestial garment.... "[35]

Phoebe has the same kind of settling effect on Holgrave.
She too was described as like an angel, childlike in her
innocence. She was "a religion in herself, warm, simple,
true with a substance that could walk on earth, and a spirit
that was capable of heaven." Her influence was to give
Holgrave a center place of stability; for example, he had

advocated building houses anew every generation, so that there
would be a continual renewal and change, but after he married
her he spoke of building a solid stone house. He was con-
scious of the change in his attitude and noted, "you find me
a conservative already." He looked to her stability to be
"more powerful than any oscillating tendency of mine."[36]

Hester is not so interchangeable with a Stowe heroine.
She is called an angel, a sister of mercy, but is more passionate and rebellious than any HBS character. Hester was
capable of committing adultery with the minister Dimmesdale
and of encouraging him to leave his pulpit to escape to
Europe to be reunited with her and their illegitimate
daughter Pearl. Hers is a stronger character than her
lover's; she acts to free him from the malevolent machina-
tions of her husband, Roger Chillingsworth. Dimmesdale,
like Kenyon and Holgrave, recognizes her greater stability
and groundedness. He pleaded, "Think for me, Hester. Thou
art strong. Resolve for me!" He longs for her presence,
"so powerful is she to sustain, so tender to soothe!" But
what she advocated is sinful because of her marriage bonds
to the wicked Chillingsworth. Dimmesdale's death saves them
from further error. Hawthorne looks to a woman with Hester's
depth of feeling, but less scarred by sorrow, to institute
a new kind of relationship between men and women. He pre-
dicts that, "the angel and apostle of the coming revelation
must be a woman..." who will act through "the ethereal medium of joy; and showing how sacred love should make us
happy."[37]

Hawthorne develops the theme of women's powers to civilize through their innocent angelic beauty, piety, and
strength of character, as was common for nineteenth century
authors. Another obvious example of the major thesis about
women's influence occurs in Mark Twain's *Tom Sawyer* where
Huck is taken over by the Widow Douglas, who "introduced him

into society--no, dragged him into it, hurled him into it."[38]
She sent him to church and to school, dressed him neatly,
and insisted that he eat and bathe regularly. Twain,
although mocking women's civilizing activities, notes their
influence.

Stowe is different from other novelists in her emphasis
that her heroines not only provide men with the orderly bonds
of society but they also provide men with a requisite link to
heaven and to grace. She saw women as more spiritual than
men so that pious women's "control...over men is like that of
the soul over the body."[39] The most overt example of a soul
saver was her character Dolly whom she described as "exhorting
with a degree of fervor and fluency in reciting texts of
Scriptures...."[40] Another one of her characters explains,
"I believe it is woman who holds faith in the world. I'd
rather have my wife's ...opinion of the meaning of a text of
Scripture than all the doctors of divinity."[41] She builds
on the theme of angelic womanhood to create the belief that
women are necessary for men to achieve spiritual awareness,
although women can achieve it through their own refined
natures without any outside teachings from men (such as Mary
(MW), Mara (Pearl), and Dolly (PP)).

HBS' EPISCOPALIANISM

HBS' turn to the Episcopalian Church can also be viewed
as part of her Romantic world view. Romanticism's influence
on religion was a gothic movement with emphasis on aesthetic
liturgy, high church forms, belief in the validity of mys-
teries, and nostalgic interest in medieval history as manifested in the Oxford movement in the Anglican Church.[42]
Romantic Christians also tended to believe that only a
Christian can have true feeling.[43]

Another facet of HBS' Romanticism was revealed in her
interest in historical tradition and fascination with medieval forms. HBS spoke of the apostolic lineage of the church,

and was fascinated with "that mysterious and awful power
that had come down from distant ages." She also saw the
Episcopal Church as continuing the rituals of the primitive
church: "I think it is fortunate that the Romish and Episcopal Churches are bringing us, descendants of the Puritans,
back to those primitive customs," one of her characters
asserts.[44] She was intrigued by the institution of sister-
hoods: in *We and Our Neighbors* she portrayed an idealized
Episcopalian sisterhood, the Sisters of St. Barnabus, who
wore crosses, practiced a highly ritualized religion, and
lived the life of poverty devoted to the care of the poor.

HBS' highest word of praise for the Episcopal Church
was her description of it as "a nice old motherly church,
that sings to us, and talks to us, and prays with us."[45]
She saw the church as a healing balm of beauty, tradition
and security.

Stowe was a mirror of her time. The same kind of Roman-
tic tendencies in religion were moving Americans such as
Orestes Brownson, a Unitarian convert to Catholicism, and
John Nevin and Philip Schaff, who emphasized the historical
development and traditional liturgy of the Church of the
German Reformed Mercersburg Seminary (established in
Mercersburg, Pennsylvania in 1836). The movement at
Mercersburg was among the first in the United States to
advocate German idealism and Schleiermacher's teaching of
the corporate nature of Christianity and its roots in his-
tory. Romantic consciousness of historical development
replaced the static orthodoxy of New England theology.[46]
Authors of novels and works of history, such as Irving,
Longfellow, Hawthorne, and Parkman also expressed nostalgia
for the Catholic past.

Her Andover neighbors suspected HBS of Episcopalian
leanings; they noticed that she had a cross in her bedroom
and one on her son Henry's grave. A letter to her daughter

Hattie shows these suspicions to have been justified: she
wrote that "our denomination does you harm," and that she
wished her daughter to join the Episcopal Church. Its sacraments would bring her "comfort and rest and peace."[47]

When she moved to Hartford she joined the twins in
attendance at the Episcopal Church. Her other daughter married an Episcopal priest.[48] In Hartford she was free to
attend the church of her choice because her husband was no
longer affiliated with a Presbyterian or Congregational college and her father was no longer living. Later in life she
returned to the Congregational fold to attend the church of
her minister son, Charles.

Charles explained that his mother left the church of
her youth in order to attend the same communion as her daughters. However, her reasons were more profound. The Episcopal Church service was the natural extension of her Romanticism: HBS considered its beautiful liturgy the best means
by which to touch the souls of poor whites and blacks, and
as soothing nurture for those on the "rebound" from New
Divinity. The evening prayer which states, "He pardoneth
and absolveth all them that truly repent and unfeignedly
believe his holy gospel," suited her notion of salvation as
did the litany which stated that God "despiseth not the
sighing of a contrite heart, nor the desire of such as be
sorrowful...." She was impressed by its stately upper class
stability and serenity. Furthermore, the church was embraced
by other women in her family, Roxana and Catharine in
particular.

Anglican theology suited her ideas of salvation better
than Calvinist Puritan theology. Anglicans had more faith
in human capacities to choose for good; they believed that
people were not as wounded by the Fall as Puritans claimed.
Anglicans believed that human reason was intact, while Puritans held that all human faculties were corrupt. Anglicans

offered hope through the primacy of sacraments as a channel
for grace--communion was available for all who wished it--
and through the forgiveness of a merciful Christ on Judgment
Day. Following Luther rather than Calvin, they taught of
the love of Jesus rather than the absolute sovereignty of a
wrathful God, mercy rather than impartial justice.[49]

She did not accept the church without reservations, however, partly because she believed that denominations were
not as significant as the invisible church, which she
believed was composed of all true believers, including Roman
Catholics. She rejected Episcopal claims to being the only
true church with the authority of their bishops stemming from
apostolic succession. Nor did she accept the church's claims
of authority about dogma; she preferred Calvinism and Puritanism which "wakes up your reason" and kindles the thinking
of the laity.[50] She found Episcopal sermons dull since it
was not as crucial for them to stir the thinking processes
of the parishioners, for these people relied on the decrees
of bishops to establish doctrine and ritual practices. Her
ideal church would be a conglomerate of Anglican ritual and
Puritan theology of Cotton Mather. The composite "Evangelical Catholicism" of her contemporary, the Episcopal priest
William Muhlenberg, approached this ideal.

HBS' affinity for the Episcopal Church was grounded in
her childhood visits to her mother's family in Nutplains;
visits which she considered the "golden hours" of her life.
Here they retained the memory of Roxanna. The children
always chose to attend the Episcopal service in Nutplains
because it seemed an integral part of the place. In addition, their Grandmother Foote read prayers every evening.
In the morning their Aunt Harriet taught them the Anglican
catechism.

Lyman disapproved of the Episcopal Church during his
struggle against the disestablishment of the Congregational

Church in Connecticut. He was opposed to its accepting members to communion without requiring the conviction of sin
and the experience of saving grace. He also was resentful
of the church for not accepting his ordination as valid.
Later, when he had realized the advantages of the voluntary
church, his judgment softened. Lyman had no objection to
his son Thomas attending Episcopal services in Philadelphia
because, he said, "The Episcopal Church is as good as any....
Your mother loved the Episcopal Church."[51] Whatever Roxanna
loved was respected by her family.

     Catharine joined her mother's church, praising it for
its acceptance to communion of those who, like herself and
Harriet, were of good character but could not produce the
necessary proof of conviction of sin and salvation. In a
book published in 1864, Catharine described the church as
wise for its acceptance of the children of church members.
Catharine made this judgment based

> on the assumption that they are lambs of Christ's
> fold and that the "Grace" needful to their suc-
> cessful training for heaven will be bestowed in
> exact proportion to the faithfulness of parents
> and children in striving to understand and obey
> the teaching of Christ.[52]

Like the theologian Horace Bushnell with his theory of
Christian nurture, Catharine and Harriet held that children
could be taught to love their heavenly father by the example
of their earthly parents. They could be trained in Christian
life without experiencing a radical transformation from the
path of sin to that of virtue.

     HBS found her roots in the Episcopal Church with not
only her sister, mother, and daughters, but also with her
beloved Puritans. She claimed that the Bay Colony under
Governors Winthrop and Dudley was warmly attached to the
Church of England: it was "their dear mother in the common
salvation, they had suckled from her breasts."[53] She

believed that it was politics that drove the Puritans from
England and that later the oppressive royal Governor Andros
increased the prejudice against Anglicans with his dictatorial
establishment of an Anglican church in Boston.[54]

HBS could also feel at home in the church because of its
strong evangelical faction. During the antebellum period the
evangelical party of the Episcopal Church was more influential than the High Church party. Both were eager to assert
their Protestant distance from the Roman Church. The evangelical wing became especially prominent after 1840 when fear
of Roman Catholic immigrants augmented suspicion of the Anglo-
Catholic Tractarian movement. The evangelicals were dominant
in the most rapidly expanding parishes. The Episcopal evangelists, like the New School Presbyterians, believed in the
importance of missionary activity, in preaching to produce
conversion, participation in interdenominational voluntary
associations, the need for the experience of regeneration,
and emphasis on scriptural authority rather than that of
church tradition. For both parties services were austere:
the word "altar" was avoided, the priest was robed in plain
white cloth, crosses and candles were infrequent, communion
was given infrequently, and the pulpit was placed in the most
prominent position. Conservative High Churchmen, led by
Bishop Henry Hobart of New York, were also against elaborate
ritual and abhorred "popish" practices. The first extensive
use of ritual was practiced by William Muhlenberg in his
school for Episcopal boys in the late 1830s but was not widespread. Ritual was, however, appealing to HBS' aesthetic
sense. Elaborate liturgy was pleasing to her, unlike her
anti-Roman Catholic contemporaries who feared it.

HBS was drawn to the church because it offered fulfillment for her Romantic desires for an aesthetic and traditional
church service. In her novels she praised the church liturgy
as enticingly beautiful, poetic, and sweet. In novels written after she joined the church many characters voiced her

attraction to Episcopalianism. St. John *(Neighbors)* was
raised a New Hampshire Calvinist; "on the rebound" he became
an Episcopal priest in New York. His poetic nature made him
dissatisfied with his childhood religion. Stowe explained
that, "It was his ideality that inclined him from the barren
and sterile chillness of New England dogmatism to the picturesque forms and ceremonies of a warmer ritual."[55]   He
conducted his liturgy with elaborate ritual: communion every
Sunday and Saint's day, prayers and psalms in the morning and
evening, candles, and elaborate Christmas and Easter rituals.

In the same novel Harry liked the church service because
he was "aesthetic" and believed that there should be more
processions, chants, and ceremonies in American churches.
Dolly, in Stowe's semi-autobiographical novel *Poganuc People*,
was drawn to the Episcopal Christmas service with its candles
and choir. Dolly joined the church as an adult when she
married an English Anglican. She felt greatly moved by the
church service, especially the music--the choir, the organ,
the singing of the Te Deum, which she said, "took me up to
the very gates of heaven. I felt as if I was hearing the
angels sing...."[56]

Stowe ridiculed fears of Popish ritual. Her despicable,
meddling character Maria Wouvermans, a Low Church Episcopalian, exclaims, "I do hate the Catholics"--obviously Stowe
did not.[57] Maria was horrified, for example, by St. John's
use of candles and felt he was very dangerous in his Catholic leanings. Her Episcopal priest also berated St. John
for his Catholic practices, but the former put his parishioners to sleep with his continual warnings against Romish
abominations, his defense of the status quo, and his uninspired preaching. Stowe did not share his fears. She was
influenced by her European travels in Catholic France and
Italy, and by her fascination with the beauty of cathedrals
and the hoary relics.[58]

St. John was reacting to "the dry husks of doctrinal
catechism," as was HBS. She used St. John and Esther Avery
(OTF) to express her attachment to the warm old motherly
church of Roxanna. Stowe explained that the church attracted
"gentle spirits, cut and bleeding by the sharp crystals of
doctrinal statement, and courting the balm of devotional
liturgy and the cool shadowy indefiniteness of more aesthetic forms of worship."[59] St. John and Esther Avery both
reacted against the insistence on conviction of sin, mirror-
ing the plight of Catharine and Harriet.

Esther was an angelic, pious woman, but since she had
not experienced conversion, she was not a Christian in the
eyes of her loving minister father. She had tried with all
her powers to be saved but had failed, boggled by her intense
intellectual processes. She was a guilty sinner according to
the theology preached by her father, that of Bellamy and
Hopkins. She became bitter, and asked why, if she were born
with a sinful nature, was it her fault that she could not
achieve conversion by her own intense efforts? She was
saved by HBS' salvation formula--LOVE. Esther fell in love
with Harry, an Anglican, whose nature was the reverse of
hers. His religion was of the heart and intuitions, "not a
formula of the head." He believed that a child could be
raised to love God by the loving example of his or her
parents. His love for Esther transfigured her and proved her
salvation: "She was like one carried away by a winged spirit,
lifted up and borne heavenward by his faith and love."[60]
HBS, like Esther, joined the Episcopal Church for its open
acceptance of those who loved Christ.

Stowe saw the church as a restorative to those "wearied
with the intense and noisy clangor of modern thought."[61] To
her the church was dignified, definite, fixed, and positive.
Stately people worshipped there, she observed. And, despite
its upper class membership, HBS believed that the Episcopal

Church was best able to minister to the poor and the blacks.
Ritual and symbol were used by the early church; she
explained that the beauty of an elaborate ritual created a
sensitivity in uneducated parishioners that prepared them for
the appreciation of spiritual beauties.

HBS attempted to put her conviction into practice by
founding an Episcopal Church for freedmen in Mandrin,
Florida. She corresponded with the Bishop of Florida and
attempted to persuade one of her brothers to change his
affiliation and preach in her church. However, southern
blacks left the Episcopal Church after the war and joined
the Methodists or Baptists, partly because the Episcopal
Church had not taken a stand against slavery in order to
avoid schism between southern and northern members.

Stowe gave up the Episcopal Church to attend her son
Charles' Congregational Church. She was not being inconsis-
tent, for her creed was that denominations are man-made. She
was in her view like her character Harry (in *Neighbors*) whom
she described as a latitudinarian. The true church was available and composed of true believers everywhere: it existed,
she wrote, "in the heart of Puritan and Ritualist alike."

She was critical of the church's authoritarian claim to
be the true church. Only her narrow-minded Episcopalian
characters--who do not express her views--claim that there
is only one true church (e.g., Mr. Coan in *PP* and Miss Debby
in *OTF*). St. John made the error of granting too much
authority to church tradition, refusing to doubt or question
church dogma and referring always to the "catacombs or the
Middle Ages or in Edward the Sixth's time."[62] Harriet
warned of the dangers of superstition and idolatries of the
past and of St. John's "monomania of veneration." He was
saved from his extremism by HBS' consistent solution of marriage to a good woman who provided a balance to her mate's
character. Sensible Angelica kept her husband balanced and

safe from idolatry. HBS believed that Puritanism was admir-
able in its promotion of the use of reason; she also praised
the Puritans for their stark courage in giving up every sensuous aid to directly face the "solemn questions of existence
and destiny in their simple nakedness."[63] One of its techniques for stirring the people was its emphasis on effective
preaching; in contrast she found Episcopal sermons dull.[64]

Her other critique of the church was its refusal to
take a stance against slavery in order to keep southern parishes in the church. Though there were some Episcopalians
who opposed slavery--such as William Steward and Solomon
Chase--they represented a minority viewpoint. HBS was enam-
ored with the beauty of its service and approved of its open
acceptance of members but she could not accept Episcopalianism with total conviction because of its authoritarianism and
its inability to stimulate the thinking of its listeners.

The faith to which she gave consistently dedicated allegiance was the spiritual grace taught by a Christian mother,
with Roxanna Beecher as model. Romanticism provided the
language for her veneration of feminine love and reliance on
the heart more than intellect. Romanticism gave her the
vocabulary to attack New England theology and freed her from
paralyzing inability to match its requirements. With her
new sense of confidence she tackled the institution of
slavery.

NOTES

[1]McLoughlin, *The Meaning of Henry Ward Beecher*, p. 28.
Cross, *Autobiography of Lyman Beecher*, V. 1, p. 44.

[2]Quoted in William McLoughlin, *The Meaning of Henry
Ward Beecher*, p. 76.

[3]Both Harriet's and Henry's marital lives fell a bit
short of the ideal: Henry's wife was undemonstrative much
like the second Mrs. Beecher, so it is likely that he found
love with several of his parishioners' wives; and Harriet
wrote to her husband Calvin that, above all, she longed to
hear him tell her that he loved her, he being preoccupied
with his biblical studies, his attacks of melancholia, and
their poor financial straits at Lane Theological Seminary.

[4]McLoughlin, *The Meaning of Henry Ward Beecher*, p. 38.

[5]Leslie Fielder, *Love and Death in the American Novel*,
p. 13.

[6]Other Romantic authors were Jane Austen, The Brontë
sisters, Elizabeth Browning and Emily Dickinson. Eighteenth
century prominent authors were Fanney Burney and Maria
Edgeworth.

[7]William McLoughlin, *The American Evangelicals* (New
York: Harper & Row, 1968), p. 14. The evangelicals popularized the glorification of home and mother and made it one
of the "main characteristics of American sentimentalism."
They did this partly in reaction to the harsh qualities of
the masculine realm of competitive business and politics
(Ibid., p. 18).

[8]Timothy Smith, *Revivalism and Social Reform* (New York:
Abingdon Press, 1957), p. 144.

[9]HBS, *Old Town Folks*, V. 2, p. 57.

[10]She shared the evangelical goal of saving souls, but
did not see revivalism as the major avenue for salvation.
Her character Nina questioned whether revival excesses
didn't do harm, but was asked in return, what forms of

religion do not? (*Dred*, vol. 1, p. 320). She was pleased
with the conventions of Christians in America and Europe who
met to pray for the gift of the Holy Spirit, "to enable them
to witness for Christ," but this was not her primary concern.

[11]HBS, *Poganuc People*, p. 91.

[12]Charles Stowe, *Harriet Beecher Stowe*, p. 314 (Letter,
7 November 1856).

[13]HBS, *Dred*, pp. 341-2.

[14]HBS, *Religious Sketches and Poems*, p. 338.

[15]HBS to Charles, 28 September 1873, Folder 186,
Schlesinger Archives.

[16]HBS, *We and Our Neighbors*, p. 204.

[17]Ibid., p. 183.

[18]HBS, *The Pearl of Orr's Island*, p. 391.

[19]Fields, *The Life and Letters of Harriet Beecher Stowe*,
p. 39.

[20]*The Complete Poetical Works of Lord Byron*, (New York:
MacMillan Co., 1907), pp. 355-356.

[21]She blamed Byron's incestuous love affair with his
half-sister for destroying his marriage with his noble, pious
and long-suffering wife. (HBS in turn was attacked as a
pornographer.)

[22]Crozier, *The Novels of Harriet Beecher Stowe*, pp. 209
and 214.

[23]HBS' positive male figures are never associated with
sexuality; only one kiss that I know of is described: an
"electric" one between Nabby and Nell in *Poganuc People*
(p. 34). This fear of intercourse and its preliminaries is
partly to be understood in light of lack of birth control.
Children were not the boon to urban dwellers that they were
to farmers. Another explanation is the vast separation

between the spheres of men and women. Women gave a great
deal of love to other women while men and women viewed each
other as an "alien" group. Women's letters to each other
sound like the utterances of romantic love, as collected by
Carroll Smith-Rosenberg ("The Female World of Love and
Ritual," *Signs*, V. 1, No. 1, (Autumn 1975), pp. 1-29). The
latter explanation is more meaningful because during the
colonial era sexuality was accepted without prudery. This
was due partly to the realistic teachings of Luther and
Calvin of marriage as a remedy for those not gifted with the
rare ability to be celibate. They also grew to emphasize
marriage as a vocation and school for character. (See
Georgia Harkness, *Women in Church and Society*, (Nashville:
Abingdon Press, 1972, p. 83). John Adams, for example,
brought his fiancée a "draft" for "as many kisses, and as
many Hours of your Company after 9 o'Clock." However, in
1827 his grandson was pleased that he thought of his fiancée
without sensual feelings (Smith, *Daughters of the Promised
Land*, pp. 69, 71).

[24]Charles Stowe, Lyman Stowe, *Harriet Beecher Stowe*,
p. 20.

[25]Sir Walter Scott, *Ivanhoe*, (Boston: Estes & Lauriat,
1893), V. 1, p. 147 and V. 2, p. 12. Part of the reason for
Scott's idealization of women (and actor David Garrick,
d. 1779) was reaction against the immorality of Georgian
aristocracy.

[26]Ibid., V. 2, p. 12.

[27]Charles E. Stowe, *Harriet Beecher Stowe*, p. 67 (Letter,
1 May 1833).

[28]Fields, *Life and Letters of Harriet Beecher Stowe*,
p. 28.

[29]Jacques Barzun, *Classic, Romantic and Modern*, (New
York: Doubleday and Co., 1961), p. 75.

[30]Fiedler, *Love and Death in the American Novel*, p. 49.

[31]Rourke, *Trumpets of Jubilee*, p. 99. Fiedler, *Love
and Death in the American Novel*, p. 262.

[32]Brown, *The Sentimental Novel in America*, pp. 285,
287-288.

[33]Even the radical feminist Elizabeth Cady Stanton opted for idealism rather than realism; she wrote in her diary: "I should rather have some pen portray the ideal woman, and paint a type worthy of our imitation." Gail Parker, ed., *The Oven-Birds*, (New York: Doubleday & Co., 1972), p. 11.

[34]See William Taylor, *Cavalier and Yankee*, (London: W. H. Allen, 1963).

[35]Nathaniel Hawthorne, *The Marble Faun*, (Boston: Houghton, Mifflin, 1903), pp. 350, 351.

[36]Hawthorne, *The House of the Seven Gables*, (Boston: Houghton, Mifflin, 1900), pp. 243, 461, 448.

[37]Hawthorne, *The Scarlet Letter*, (New York: Bigelow, Brown, 1923), pp. 188, 206, 269.

[38]Mark Twain, *The Adventures of Tom Sawyer*, (New York: Harper & Bro., 1903), p. 315.

[39]HBS, *My Wife and I*, p. 33.

[40]HBS, *Poganuc People*, p. 118.

[41]HBS, *My Wife and I*, p. 97.

[42]See James Hastings Nicholes, *Romanticism in American Theology, Nevin and Schaft at Mercersburg*, (Chicago: Univ. of Chicago Press, 1961).

[43]George Mosse, *The Culture of Western Europe*, (New York, Rand McNally Co., 1961), p. 38.

[44]HBS, *My Wife and I*, p. 297.

[45]HBS, *Old Town Folks*, V. 1, p. 36.

[46]Mary Ryan, "American Society, and The Cult of Domesticity," p. 3.

[47]HBS to Hattie, January 1862, Folder 113, Schlesinger Archives.

[48]However, Georgianna continued to suffer from despair about her salvation and what her mother described as "religious melancholy." HBS to Hattie, 16 August 1876, Folder 160, Schlesinger Archives.

[49]John New, *Anglican and Puritan: The Basis of Their Opposition*, (Stanford, California: Stanford Univ. Press, 1964), pp. 6, 72.

[50]HBS, *Old Town Folks*, v. 1, p. 362.

[51]Cross, ed., *The Autobiography of Lyman Beecher*, V. 2, p. 379.

[52]*Religious Training of Children in the School, The Family, and The Church*, (New York: Harper, 1864), as quoted in Foster, *The Rungless Ladder*, p. 180.

[53]HBS, *Old Town Folks*, V. 1, p. 413.

[54]Increase Mather illustrated the resentment against the Anglicans when he described its service as Romish and idolatrous, with "broken responds and shreds of prayer which the priests and people toss between them like tennis balls." James Addison, *The Episcopal Church in the United States*, (Hamden, Conn.: Archon Books, 1969), p. 41.

[55]HBS, *We and Our Neighbors*, p. 335.

[56]HBS, *Poganuc People*, p. 256.

[57]Wilson believed that HBS almost became a Roman Catholic while in Rome in 1856 but offered no proof. *Crusader in Crinoline*, p. 56. See my Appendix 2 on High Church Episcopalianism.

[58]She described her attraction to the Roman Catholic Churches, but was horrified by the splendiferous display of Pope and Cardinals as not representative of Christ. Also she was a product of her upbringing, feeling "a kind of Puritan tremor of conscience at witnessing such a theatrical pageant on the Sabbath." But she defended "Hebrew ritualism" (referring to temple rituals) as instituted by God. HBS, *Sunny Memories of Foreign Lands*, V. 2, p. 329.

[59]HBS, *Old Town Folks*, V. 2, p. 14.

[60]Ibid., V. 2, p. 87.

[61]HBS, *We and Our Neighbors*, p. 95.

[62]Ibid., p. 449.

[63]HBS, *Poganuc People*, p. 215.

[64]The church itself realized that it was not reaching
the common people, that it needed better preaching. In 1853
a bishop described sermons as "read in a dull, cold, prosy
manner, and monotonous in tone, and often very lengthy."
(Addison, *The Episcopal Church in the United States*, p. 182.

CHAPTER FIVE

SALVATION APPLIED TO SLAVERY

REASONS FOR REFORM

Romantic sentimentalism in religion and literature was potentially a feminist attack on orthodoxy. It gave women a means by which to create fictional heroines when none was available among their contemporaries embroidering in their parlors. The intensity of their feelings, their "sacred rage," provided them a basis for equality and attacks on injustice. Women organized reform organizations which were quasi-religious with opening prayers and fervent hymn singing. Organizational outlets for women's righteous passions were reform movements such as abolition, church ladies' aid societies and temperance groups.[1]

The Romantic cult of love added to a humanitarian revaluation of ethical values resulting in reform movements. As HBS explained, "the best offering of love...is doing for others" and that work for anti-slavery and temperance was part of the gospel of Christ.[2] Other legacies of her religious inheritance propelled her toward activism. The first influence was the Puritan radical judgment on the world, seen as the battleground with Satan, in contrast to the Anglican and Episcopal tendency to preserve the status quo as traditional institutions were viewed as basically good.[3] Lyman Beecher, for example, frequently used battle imagery such as the need to form reform societies where every member is a soldier in a "moral militia."[4] A second inheritance was from Jonathan Edwards who stressed the marks of conversion as sweetness and missionary outreach to others by the "visible saints." The evangelical preparation for the millenium led to a proliferation of interdenominational voluntary reform associations since sin, Lyman Beecher explained, was anti-social.

The faith in the second coming of Christ in the New
World was linked with a fervent nationalistic belief in God's
special covenant with America as the New Zion, a light to
the world. This belief was first promulgated by the Puritans, then was restated by Protestant Federalist, Whig, and
Republican politicians and clergy. Protestant reformers
were anxious about the future of the nation divided by
immigrants, emigrants to wilderness areas, the growth of
cities, and sectional antagonisms. The future of the nation
and of Christianity were linked by the reformers who, like
HBS, believed that, "The American government is the only
permanent republic which ever based itself upon the principles laid down by Jesus Christ,"[5] and like Lyman that civil
magistrates are also ministers of God.[6] He believed that
social reform and revivalism went hand in hand holding his
paper on temperance reform to be the most important one he
ever wrote. Thus Harriet, through her reform work with her
pen--a work deemed natural to pious women--could join the
ranks of the "moral militia" led by her father. HBS fought
for emancipation of slavery while maintaining a conviction
of innate differences between blacks and whites, a kind of
noblese oblige. By today's standards she would be judged a
racist and an elitist.

The Beechers associated the preservation of American
republican institutions with the inculcation of Protestant
morality. They naturally supported the Federalists, then
the Whigs, and finally the Republicans, as these parties
believed that the federal government should enforce Protestant morality. New England was a power base for these
parties. The Beechers scorned the Jeffersonians and
Jacksonians who assumed a more laissez-faire attitude and
who were villified as atheists.[7]

HBS recounted her father's struggle against religious
toleration in Connecticut in *Poganuc People* and reflected

some of his political attitudes in *Old Town Folks*. She was
sympathetic and supportive of his deeply ingrained Federalist
fear of the influence of French Revolutionary thought. Her
character Emily Rossiter was corrupted by embracing French
Deism in reaction to the ultra-Calvinist teachings of her
youth. She reaped the ultimate degradation of bearing a
child out of wedlock. Repentant, she "learned from the
French Revolution how mistaken had been those views of human
progress which come from mere unassisted reason, when it
rejects the guidance of revealed religion."[8] HBS rejected
Deism as alien to the high purposes which brought her Puritan
ancestors to the New World.

Consistent with Federalist Francophobia, she associated
the Jeffersonian party with Jacobinism. She mirrored the
superior attitude of her father and his party in her narrator's description of the Democrats' appeal to the lower
classes: the Democrats "wanted the control of the state;
and if rabid, drinking, irreligious men would give it to them,
why not use them after their kind? When the brutes had won
the battle for them, they would take care of the brutes, and
get them back into the stall."[9] HBS was never ready to condemn a whole group so she explained through her narrator
that there were good people who were Democrats. She shared
Lyman's critique of the aristocratic trappings of the Federalists as when she portrayed a reactionary character,
Miss Debby *(OTF)*, who dismissed her servant for attending a
primary election meeting.

The Beechers all shared in the conviction that they
were doing God's work and preparing for the golden age to
come. The enemy changed but the Beecher arrogance did not
nor did their concept of being a part of the messianic group
of erudite descendants of New England Puritans. Their attitude was like that of the younger generation of Federalists
who, from 1800-1816, advocated a silent and covert elite

group to lead the populace. Lyman prayed in a Cincinnati
sermon: "Oh Lord, grant we may not despise our rulers and
grant that they may not act so, that we can't help it."[10]
Educated ministers, he believed, were needed to preserve
American political institutions.

    HBS shared in the conviction that people like her family
had a mission to help prepare America for the millenium.
She shared in their horror of Jacobin infidels, mobocracy
and barbarism, but mainly channeled her energies into preaching of the home and family as the nexus for salvation, rather
than reform societies, law codes, or the efforts of clergy.
She believed in the power of female descendants of Puritans,
for the men had lost their power in endless petty theological disputes. She hoped that when they had been further
educated the women could refine governmental processes corrupted by men--but salvation was primarily gained in the
woman's sphere of the home.

THE NEW ENGLAND PROTESTANT REFORMERS

    Reform was to be led by an elite suited by their descent
from Anglo-Saxon New England Puritans. Like her fellow
Romantics she was fascinated by the differences between
peoples and nations; she subscribed to sharp character differences between Anglo-Saxons, Celts, and Africans. In her
New England chauvinism mystically seated racial qualities
far outweighed differences generated by environment or history. Harriet joined in the Beecher belief that the blood
line of the Puritan "race" was the basis of the ideal community of which Boston with its "sacred" associations was
the capital and "consecrated ground."[11]

    Harriet's affection for colonial New England was more
than genteel nostalgia: in its history she saw a living
ideal. She shared her father's belief that it was probably
the most perfect state of society. It was for her like the

record of Old Testament society, centered on its marriages
and its progeny, whose sons and daughters would outshine
Moses and Esther, augmented by New Testament teachings.

Her Puritan City of God was theological, moral, thrifty,
grave and thoughtful, with an educated populace, without
paupers, and with negligible crime. It gathered together
the best of the Hebraic and classic traditions. New England
was for the new republic what the "Dorian hive" was for
Greece: the conscience, brains, and heart of the nation.

For Harriet the City of God was no accidental construct.
It had nothing to do with the social chaos of Jacksonian
mobocracy: Nature legislated class distinctions that divided the "best families," the "haute noblesse," the "proud
democracy" from the lower classes of the "ill-educated,
improvident, and foolish."[12] Although in *Dred* she suggests
a past utopia in which there were no classes and everyone
worked, those times had faded with the advent of immigrants
and foreigners. *Poganuc People*, her fictional account of
Litchfield life, describes Harriet's ideal world as regulated
by benign and natural class divisions. Her fiction is popu-
lated with wealthy families, especially New Yorkers and
Southerners, whose genius lay in their blood lines, such as
St. Clare, the Claytons, Van Arsdales, Van Astrachans, and
Seymours. Dolly, her own semi-autobiographical character,
is a country girl certified into this world by marrying "a
rich handsome feller." For Harriet class structure was a
corollary of Puritan chauvinism: It was the wealthy families
of established lineage who were "solid planted artillery on
the walls of our zion in these days of dissolving views."[13]

Henry Ward Beecher's preachment of the Genteel Tradition helps to illuminate his famous sister's class and
racial biases. Where their father had exhorted the wealthy
to support missionaries and tract societies, Henry would
finger precious gems and talk of the "ministry of beauty,"

of the building of mansions and parks. His gospel of
refined beauty was another vehicle of class distinction, for,
he would explain, the experience of beauty was an inherited,
aristocratic faculty, and one could not make an apple out of
a potato. Henry's delicate aestheticism is the counterpart
to Harriet's reformist zeal: both interpreted the Protestant
elevation of the soul to salvation as a divine call for elite
leadership of the lower, degraded classes. For example,
Henry's novel *Norwood* juxtaposes a genteel, sensitive, spiritual heroine against the brutish black Pete Sawmill who is
portrayed with animal or child imagery.

   Norwood underlines the relationship between the Beecher
racial and class ideology and the growing immigrant domination of the cities. It contrasts the purity of rural white
Protestant New England with the corruption and vice prevalent among the foreigners and Catholics of the cities.
Norwood provides a literary footnote to the first great WASP
defection from the cities, when as the Boston patricians lost
their influence to political machines based on immigrant
Irish votes they began their post-Civil War retreat to the
estates which still populate the North Shore. The retreat
was accompanied by the construction of new "walls of zion":
country clubs, boarding schools and resorts.

   Regarding her concern for women, Stowe explained in
Pink and White Tyranny that it was urban women--not the
virtuous country women--who perused the modern, hot, sensuous
French novels. Moreover the city produced a people she
described as jaded, sated, blasé, indolent and hurried, caring more for emotion than reason. New York City was a "great
red dragon" growing wild and unchecked. It was a degenerate
age, shunning the "strait and narrow ways of self-denial" as
practiced by the Puritans.

   Though the early Puritans had produced a special race of
women who were physically, intellectually, and spiritually

strong, each successive generation wandered further from the
path of virtue, producing a modern city girl who was frail,
nervous, languid, and flirty, going so far as to toy with
the sacred institution of marriage. Stowe noted they counted
marriage offers as an Indian did scalps.[14] Girls who were
raised in the country far from the corroding influence of
the dragon could more easily assimilate the New England
traits. For example, Grace *(PWT)*, although she was living
in the Gilded Age, could benefit from her family's training
in the "kindly severe discipline of Puritan New England,"
acting from high principle and frequent self-examination.
At the heart of this training was the belief that marriage
was the holiest of all duties.

More than merely possessing a set of ideals, the Puritans were a "consecrated race."[15] Hence their descendants
were a special breed. As her brother Henry stated, "It
seems to me that Puritan blood means blood touched with
Christ's blood."[16] HBS saw descendants of the Puritans as
"true-blue" families who formed a nobility, characterized
by their noblesse oblige and their literary interests.[17]
For example, in *My Wife and I*, Ida was proof of the distinction of Puritan lineage, for she was "as bent on testifying
and going against the world as any old Covenanter." Her
sister Eva was also a "princess of the blood," with her
blond hair and dark eyes.[18]

The Anglo-Saxon heritage was partly responsible for
Puritan greatness. Although sometimes critical, HBS saw the
Anglo-Saxons as the superior race: she believed that they
valued truthfulness, while Celts had a predilection for
deception.[19] Anglo-Saxons are just, vigorous, hardworking,
efficient, clean and independent, cherishing liberty, as
contrasted to the Indians in *Poganuc People* who depend upon
Dolly's family for frequent meals. Only Stowe's mulattoes,
not her pure blacks, resist the bonds of slavery. St. Clare

(UTC) predicted that in a slave revolt Anglo-Saxon blood
would lead the way, that "sons of white fathers, with all
our haughty feelings burning in their veins, will not always
be bought, sold and traded."[20] In addition, they have a
kind of nontalkative levelheadedness as opposed to the
fiery nature of a Spaniard like Moses (Pearl). She pointed
out that more than half of the great men whose biographies
she compiled were from New England farm backgrounds, fully
a third direct descendants of the Pilgrim, concluding that
"blood will out."[21]

     Her belief in Anglo-Saxonism was reinforced by the
scientific dogma of the era which transformed existing cari-
catures of the lazy Negro, the drunken Irishman, and the
mercenary Jew into empirical categories.[22] Scientists had
traditionally held that all races had a common origin in
Adam and Eve, but in the nineteenth century they began to
posit separate origins of races and concomitant inequalities.
Arthur de Gobineau's Essai sur l'inégalité des races
humaines was published in America in 1856. Holding that
Aryans were distinguished by power, energy, and the ability
to lead, it called upon the theory of natural selection to
justify and account for racial superiority. Protestant
clergy took up the refrain with their stress on the superiority of the Anglo-Saxon race which they defined as of
Hebrew, Roman and Greek mixed stock, not thinking in terms
of blue-eyed blond Aryans. As early as 1837 Horace Bushnell
cautioned Americans to protect their Anglo-Saxon blood from
the immigrant tide.[23] The Anglo-Saxon movement had become
so well established by 1880 that Josiah Strong could preach
Anglo-Saxon leadership of the world.[24] The political results
of this racism were the American Protective Association,
literacy tests for immigrants, and the establishment of
quota systems for immigrants in the 1920s.

Concerned for the preservation of the thrifty Anglo-
Saxon virtues from the immigrant hordes, HBS described Puritan New England as pure, happy, free from poverty or fear of
theft when it was composed of "our own blood and race,"
when the "pauper population of Europe had not as yet been
landed upon our shores."[25] On the other hand, Aunt Maria--
who in her foolishness is generally the mouthpiece for views
disliked by Stowe--spoke with disdain of the "inroads of a
tribe of untaught barbarians."[26] Stowe was not an extremist
in her Anglo-Saxonism. And, as we are to see with the Irish
question, Stowe was much more tolerant than many of her contemporaries.

The Irish came in large numbers to eastern seaboard
cities in the 1830s and 40s escaping the terrible potato
famine. In her novels Stowe utilized some of the stereotypes, as her only portrayals of the Irish are as servants
or as the drunken father of the servant girl Maggie (Neighbors). But Stowe did not share in the nativist view of the
Irish Catholic immigration as a product of Jesuit machina-
tions to undermine American republican institutions. She
counseled the employers of Catholic servants not to try to
convert them to Protestantism and explained that there is
unity even in "opposite Christian forms," so that a Protestant mistress and a Catholic servant could work together in
harmony. The religious faith of Catholic Irish girls who
were alone in the New World kept them pure in demeanor:
this was proof for HBS that their religion should not be
tampered with. She also described the Irish girls as heroic
in their efforts to provide for themselves and also for
impoverished friends in Ireland. Yet the only Irish she
portrayed or discussed were those whom she considered lower
class, an "ignorant and uncultivated people.[27]

She refused to write of the Roman Catholic Church as
the Scarlet Woman; although the church was guilty of many

corruptions, it preserved, she wrote, the teachings necessary for salvation. An example of a true Christian is the
heroine of her novel *Agnes* set in Catholic Italy where its
heroine was as much saved and at peace "as if she had been
the veriest Puritan maiden."[28] She also pointed out that
the church had produced great spiritual leaders like Fénélon
and Thomas á Kempis in addition to its commendable missionary
work among the Indians.

Her most harsh attack on the Roman Catholic Church was
written in her *Key to Uncle Tom's Cabin*. She compared the
Catholic Church to the Southern churches which supported
slavery which she chastised for being "as truly anti-Christ
as the religion of the Church of Rome...." She also
attacked the Roman Church for its "false principles" and
"disadvantageous influences."[29] Yet she was careful to add
in the same passage that in the Roman Catholic Church there
are thousands of devoted Christians.

In other places she attacked the church for its eccle-
siasticism, which needed correction by Luther, and she
believed that in their ministry priests relied on authority
rather than reason. She was opposed to the monastic tradition which scorned marriage for the most devout and disliked
its extremes of asceticism. Her character Agnes mortified
herself with fasting and by wearing a cross with steel points
on her chest, all because a priest made her feel guilty
about her love for a man which threatened to keep her from
convent life.

The typical Protestant of the 1850s was raised from
birth to fear Catholics. Both Stowe's family and denomination were active in the anti-Catholic movement. The main
reason her father wished to settle in the Mississippi Valley
was to marshal Protestant forces against the Romish threat.
In a series of anti-Catholic sermons preached in Boston in
the 1830s Lyman outlined a Catholic alliance with European

despotic forces in a "design" to undermine American republican institutions.[30] He saw large numbers of Catholic immigrants as a threat not only to American churches but to
governmental institutions as well. Placing particular emphasis on the danger of Catholic schools attended by Protestant
students, he spoke of the schools as deliberately financed
by the European plotters to convert Protestants. To counteract the Popish menace he proposed in 1816 that there be a
school for every district, a Protestant pastor for every
thousand people, and a Bible in every home. These steps
would result, he predicted, in a "sameness of views and feelings and interests which would lay the foundation of our
empire upon a rock."[31]

     Though of strong convictions the Beechers did not go as
far as to support the Know-Nothing Party of the 1850s,[32]
whose stated aim was to "resist the insidious policy of the
Church of Rome, and other foreign influences against the
institution of our country."[33] The Beechers agreed with the
aim of the nativist party but disliked its means. Henry Ward
spoke out against the party describing it in his usual flow-
ery prose as "secret conclaves controlled by hoary knaves
versed in political intrigue."[34] During the late 1850s
sectional problems pre-empted nativism and the Beechers
shifted their concern to slavery issues.

     In contrast to her somewhat ambivalent positions con-
cerning the Irish and Catholicism, HBS rose to the defense
of the Jews, partly because of her love of Old Testament
emphasis on family life. Eva, in *We and Our Neighbors*,
visited a Jewish family and was impressed with their virtue.
This was quite a discovery and tended to invalidate Eva's
family's teaching that Jews, however scholarly or refined,
were "disreputable." Although she considered herself to be
defending and praising blacks and Jews, HBS was guilty of
racism: her blacks had the humility and docility to be good

Christians and Anglos appeared haughty and arrogant--yet
Anglos led, achieved, and produced. HBS was an elitist who
felt that descendants of Puritan stock had been given the
call to save America and her family attempted to answer that
call.

The Beecher goal of a predominantly Protestant America
with pronounced New England characteristics was achieved by
mid-century. The majority of colleges were founded by
Protestant denominations, pre-Civil War urban revivals were
widely supported and reported, and the religious press was
growing faster than the secular.[35] After the war the immigrants and the newly rich threatened the old rural mentality.
HBS wrote her novels in an attempt to counteract the influence of the city and the new power elite. Her model, goal,
and guide was the New England Puritanism of the seventeenth
century--the Arcadian time when Americans were of one blood,
touched by the blood of Christ.

HBS' ANTI-SLAVERY CRUSADE

Without *Uncle Tom's Cabin*, Abraham Lincoln could not
have been President of the United States. So, at least,
believed Charles Sumner, the eminent senator from Massachusetts. Present day scholars like James Rawley conclude that
its author was perhaps the most influential figure in the
anti-slavery reformation of the 1850s.[36] She built the myth
of woman's moral superiority and the idealization of the home
into a political weapon for reform. Stowe herself believed
that she was directly inspired by God to write *Uncle Tom's
Cabin*: "I can truly say that I write with life-blood," she
said. "The Lord himself wrote it, and I was but the hum-
blest of instruments in his hand."[37] She believed that the
churches, in ignoring or condoning slavery, had defied the
warning of Christ that "inasmuch as ye have done it to the
least of these my brethren, ye have done it unto me"
(Matthew 25:45).

HBS' rage and sorrow at the institution of slavery was
inspired in large part by her reverence for the Christian
family.[38] Because the slave codes permitted the separation
of black families, allowed the sexual abuse of black women
and by condoning illicit relations between the slavemaster
and his female minions, threatened the sanctity of white
families, she abhorred them. This fact of life was brought
home to her by her Aunt Mary, who returned from a failed
marriage in Jamaica, horrified by the mulatto offspring of
her husband. Disgusted with the narrow, pedantic disputations of the traditional theologians and inspired by the
zeal of the Romantic Era, HBS began to seek her Savior's
image in the emotions of women, children, and the humble
black folk of her fantasies.

HBS only gradually entered the crusade against slavery.
In the 1830s she criticized the militant abolitionists for
indulging in "excesses" and felt that "an intermediary
society" between slavery and freedom would be preferable to
immediate abolition. Among her family, only Edward took a
strong.stand against slavery; his position is suggested in
his *Narrative of the Riots at Alton*, 1837. In 1850, however,
with the passage of the vicious Fugitive Slave Act, abolition
became respectable in the North. Saddened by the pathetic
plight of the fugitives and angered by the dramatic and tragic incidents which ensued from the attempted rescues--one
Ohio woman murdered her daughter to save her from return to
slavery--HBS became a crusader. *Uncle Tom's Cabin* was her
outraged response.

She explained to the editor of the *National Era* in which
Uncle Tom's Cabin was serialized that she previously had felt
"no particular call to meddle with this subject."[39] Of her
four contributions to the *National Era* before *Uncle Tom's
Cabin* only one mentioned the slavery issue. She told her
readers that she had avoided reading about slavery because

it was too painful and she had believed that "advancing
light and civilization would certainly live it down."[40]

However, the Fugitive Slave Law made her realize that
progress was not being achieved. She wished that her father
would come to Boston and preach as he had in Litchfield
against the slave trade or that some Martin Luther would
rise up to correct the injustice. Her sister-in-law wrote
pleading with Harriet to write something to make the nation
feel how accursed slavery was. When she read the letter,
HBS stood up, crumpled it in her hand and told her family,
"I will if I live."[41] Her brother Henry, who held his sensa-
tional slave auctions of attractive mulatto women in his
Brooklyn church, also encouraged her to write.

She first wrote a description of Uncle Tom's death and
then began the installments of the story in June of 1851.
The book was much more lengthy than planned; she received no
extra payment but was driven to give voice to her divinely
inspired story. Her son Charles called *Uncle Tom's Cabin* a
"work of religion," which was also Harriet's view. She
believed that a major evil of slavery was its erosion of
family life, the cornerstone of American morality. In *Uncle
Tom's Cabin* Stowe gave examples of its abuses. The slave
Eliza Harris crossed the river on the ice floes alone with
her baby, separated from her husband. Cassy was sexually
abused by Legree. Mrs. St. Clare was an inadequate wife and
mother as she was spoiled by the luxury and irresponsibility
perpetuated by slavery.

HBS was obsessed by the separation of mother and child.
She explained that at the time of the death of her infant
son in a cholera epidemic, "I learned what a poor slave
mother may feel when her child is torn away from her."[42]
Her identification with slave mothers and wives aroused her
zeal and so did her evangelical background which taught her
to view life in terms of conversion. The link between

evangelist Charles Finney and his abolitionist convert
Theodore Weld is a prime example of the evangelical flavor
of abolitionism.

Another facet of Stowe's involvement in abolitionism
was the precedent set by other women. Male clergy's defense
of slavery aroused female ire and increased confidence in
women's judgments. Nathaniel Taylor, for example, hedged on
slavery and Catharine struck out at "our leading ministers
[who] take such low worldly ground...."[43] Harriet attacked
Reverend Joel Parker in *Uncle Tom's Cabin* as a Presbyterian
who justified slavery. He threatened legal action so she
deleted references to him in later editions. Sarah and
Angelina Grimké began to speak in public against slavery in
1837, first to women's church groups which soon became
"promiscuous" gatherings attended by men as well. Lydia
Maria Child published in 1833 *An Appeal in Favor of that Class
of Americans Called Africans*, which Stowe read. Child commented on slavery's splintering of families. HBS also used
Angelina and Theodore Weld's *Slavery As It Is*, which described
disruption of domesticity.[44] In Connecticut, Prudence Crandall
organized a school for black girls but it was soon closed in
a storm of racist agitation. Women were present at the founding of the American Anti-Slavery Society in December of 1833;
some addressed the group. Angelina Grimké, Abby Kelly,
Lucretia Mott, and Maria Chapman organized and led women's
anti-slavery conventions such as the one held in Philadelphia
in 1838.

Garrisonians won the appointment of Abby Kelly to the
business committee of the American Anti-Slavery Society in
1840. As a result some male members withdrew in protest and
formed the American and Foreign Anti-Slavery Society. Other
women abolitionists became prominent figures in the anti-
slavery crusade, including black heroines Harriet Tubman of
underground railroad fame, Sarah Douglass, and Sojourner

Truth, who visited HBS in Andover in 1863.[45] It has also
been suggested that women bogged down by household drudgery,
like HBS, identified their low status and powerlessness with
slavery.

Woman's frustrations found catharsis in the war effort:
it has been suggested that *Uncle Tom's Cabin* was an "orgias-
tic domestic catharsis" and the war itself a "ritualistic
purgation of the tensions of the American family."[46] The
woman's rights movements, beginning in 1848, stirred up con-
flict between the sexes. Clergy preached sermons against
un-Biblical and unsexed women and female reform leaders
denounced male defenders of slavery. Some women began to
view themselves as like slaves and their fathers and husbands
like slave masters. The rigid separation of the roles and
spheres of men and women did not leave them much in common.
Same sex friendships often seemed deepest. The war turned
attention away from the struggle for women's rights to eman-
cipating the slaves.

HBS' attitude toward slaves themselves was both conde-
scending and romantic.[47] The shade of the color of her
black characters often indicates the level of their intellect and sophistication. Stowe romanticized black people
considering them an "exotic race" with "a character so
essentially unlike the hard and dominant Anglo Saxon race."[48]
One of her blacks was "a curious contrast to everybody
around" in his gurgling, giggling joy in being alive. Her
soulful black characters, Tom, Milly *(Dred)*, and Candace
(MW) were intended to present a contrast to the white man's
convoluted religious practices. As he lay dying, Uncle Tom,
with genuine Christian compassion, forgave Simon Legree for
his sins.

Stowe's abolitionist policy was essentially conservative in *Uncle Tom's Cabin*. She advocated gradual emancipation and colonization in Liberia. George and Eliza Harris

settled in Canada, Topsy and others migrated to Africa.
None of her major characters remained to fight slavery in
America.

Nor was HBS antagonistic to the South. The slave
traders in *Uncle Tom's Cabin*, like Simon Legree, are North-
erners. She blamed the social system which ensnared the
slave owner and slave alike. Tom, for example, was sold not
because his owner was malicious but because he was in debt
to the slave traders. Although a Northerner, Miss St. Clare's
deep-seated prejudice made her dread physical contact with
Topsy. The hero St. Clare and his saintly daughter Eva were
Southerners. HBS expected attacks from the North rather than
the South because she thought "the gentle voice of Eva" proclaimed her kindly sentiments toward the South. She hoped
to appeal to the Southern conscience. The tragedies of Tom
and Eva would, she hoped, move the South to repentance.

The original intent of *Dred* (begun in February, 1856)
was to encourage the South to reform its system from within.
Clayton and his sister Anne are the models; they educate
their slaves, intending to prepare them for their emancipation. Their philosophy was that "there is to be a graduated
system of work and wages introduced--a system that shall
teach the nature and rights of property and train to habits
of industry and frugality...."[49] Clayton tells the mulatto
slave Harry to be patient and to seek repeal of unjust laws.

However, a series of events occurred while she was
writing *Dred* that dimmed her optimistic faith in the salvation of the South. The May 1856 attack on Senator Sumner
and the events in Bleeding Kansas convinced her that the
Southerners were beyond redemption. She lost her faith in
the "good people," the clergy and church elders who were
vociferous in defense of slavery. Mr. Jekyl, who looks on
"niggers" as investments, is a respected elder in the
Presbyterian Church. Her character Judge Clayton explained

that only the Quakers and coventors (a reference to Scottish
Coventers) of the South, the Freewill Baptists and a few
others in the North lifted their voices in tribute to the
teaching of Christ.

Dred was called by some of her contemporaries as an onslaught on the Christian religion. HBS did view the Christian denominations as degenerate and derelict in their
Christian duties, caring more about the unity of their church
structures than about Christian principles. She believed
that none of the denominations were willing to support an
unpopular cause; as drunkard Tom Gordon told Clayton, "There
ain't a minister in the State that will stand by you." Not
only were the churches afraid to speak out against slavery,
but they defended it. Her character Mr. Jekyl stated that
slavery was a "divinely appointed institution."[50] Their
political diffidence caused the Presbyterian General Assembly
to ignore the slavery issue; to make up for it, Stowe bit-
terly explained, they ordered a crusade against dancing.
The only thing the Church had done was to "forbid and frown."

Stowe did remain steadfast in her belief that the churches
could be the salvation of the slaves. She told Frederick
Douglas that the hope of his people was to be found in the
churches and that the anti-slavery movement "must and will
become a purely religious one."[51] She explained that the
best and most conscientious people in America were church
members. She saw the Bible and prayer as the solace of
black Christians. She chided Garrison's Liberator articles
fearing that "your paper will take from poor Uncle Tom his
Bible, and give him nothing in its place," since Garrison
was critical of Biblical references to slavery. She told
Garrison that her field of activity was the church, that she
and her brother Edward were "trying to secure a universal
arousing of the pulpit."[52] She wished to send a copy of an
anti-slavery speech given by Edward to every minister in the

country. But by the time she wrote *Dred* her faith in the
church had dwindled. She still believed that reform should
be initiated by the church through training of their members
but saw no evidence of the proper and necessary action.

Clayton is told, "Your plans for gradual emancipation,
or reform, or anything tending in that direction, are utterly
hopeless...."[53] Dred became the major character in volume
two. He was modeled on the religious visionary Nat Turner
who led a Virginia uprising in 1831 in which fifty-one whites
were killed. HBS did away with the previous central character, Nina, leaving her to the mercy of a cholera epidemic.

As a lover of the Declaration of Independence, HBS could
sympathize with a slave uprising, contemplated by Dred, but
was not ready to condone one. She had a character say:

> I admit that your people suffer under greater
> oppression than even our fathers suffered and if
> I believed that they were capable of obtaining
> and supporting a government, I should believe in
> their right to take the same means to gain it....
> I do not think that, should they make the effort,
> they would succeed. They would only embitter the
> white race against them, and destroy the sympathy
> which many are beginning to feel for their
> oppressed condition.[54]

Dred is an Old Testament prophet speaking wrath and
judgment in opposition to Tom's Christ-like turning of the
other cheek. Dred was kept from fomenting an uprising by
the Christian pacifist Milly who counseled him to leave vengeance to the Lord. HBS equivocated and left the issue of
black oppression in the air by having Clayton migrate with
his slaves to Canada to form a township. Harry Gordon also
went to Canada and Milly went to New York to engage in chari-
table work with both black and white children. Dred was
killed by slave owners so she did not have to grapple with
the unsolvable problem.

Southern reform was not the answer to the slavery problem nor was migration to Canada or Africa. War became the

answer. HBS saw in the Civil War God's holy wrath, a punishment for sin. If it is an evil, she stated in the
Independent, "it is less evil than many others and one
attended by many and high forms of good."[55] She was pleased
to see Andover theology students drilling, stating that,
"There will be no dyspeptic views of theology so far as this
generation of ministers is concerned."[56]

          HBS was critical of Lincoln's conduct of the war, as
were many others. He was too radical for the moderates and
too moderate for the radicals. He was caricatured by his
critics as a baboon, a gorilla, a Simple Susan. Lincoln's
steps toward emancipation were too slow for HBS. She spoke
out for immediate emancipation in 1861, while in his annual
address to Congress in 1862 Lincoln aimed for emancipation
by 1900, asking Congress for funds to aid states in gradual
emancipation at home and for colonization in Liberia. She
attacked his First Inaugural Address for "the coolness with
which from first to last, he ignores the existence of any
moral or religious sense as forming any element in national
movements."[57]

          Before she published her "Address to the Women of
England" in 1862, HBS went to visit Lincoln to make sure he
would "make good" on emancipation of the slaves. She
described him as being funny and droll and referred to him
as "Honest Old Abe." When the Proclamation freeing the slaves
in the rebel states was signed in January of 1863 she felt
that her mission was completed. When she heard the bells
toll for the proclamation she felt it was "the consummation
of my life's desires."[58] She came to see him as a great
soul, chosen by God as a martyr with a "fatherly heart," who
did the "greatest work that has been done in modern times."[59]
She supported Johnson's Reconstruction policies believing
that if the Negroes were oppressed in the South they could
emigrate and from her winter home in Florida she made

gestures toward helping freed slaves. She established a
church for them but her attention turned mainly to the problems of northern city life after the war.

HBS used her desk-pulpit to fight slavery which
besmirched American women and the family, was un-Christian,
and held back the coming of the millenium. Clergy and their
denominations did not assume their rightful leadership in
opposing slavery, so she chastised them, tried to mobilize
them as in her mammoth collection of clerical signatures,
visited Lincoln to spur him on, and criticized England for
her support of the South. Her absolute sense of righteousness and divine inspiration caused her to write a moralistic
novel, which could be written at home, to challenge the
Goliaths.

Notes

[1]The WCTU was one of the most powerful reform groups, directed by Francis Willard at its height from 1874 to 1898. Anti-Saloon League women invaded taverns in the 1870s, kneeling to pray for men's salvation from alcohol. Another group for Christian women, the YWCA, was formed in 1866.

[2]HBS, *Religious Studies*, p. 118.

[3]The Puritan effort to gain control of the evershifting world was also an attempt to discipline and control their anxiety about their own lives, so that when there was less to fear, Puritanism lost its appeal, according to Walzer (*Revolution of the Saints*), pp. 310 and 316.

[4]Lyman Beecher, "A Reformation of the Morals Practical and Indispensable," 1812, New Haven, in *The Reform of Society: Four Sermons, 1804-1828,* (New York: Arno Press, 1972), p. 18.

[5]HBS, *Men of Our Times*, (Hartford, Conn.: Hartford Publishers, 1868), p. 554.

[6]Lyman Beecher, *A Reformation of Morals*, p. 14.

[7]In a case study of the relation of politics/religion in Wayne County, Michigan, Formisano found that 61 percent of Whigs were Yankee Presbyterians, and that benefit societies interlocked with Whig and Presbyterian leadership. The Republican Party inherited the Whig activism and "moral ultraism," fighting for reforms in women's rights and education, slavery, temperance, etc. It was constituted by 70 percent Yankees and 67 percent of the Presbyterians were Republicans. Republicanism, through its anti-slavery stance, linked to an egalitarian tradition which had been the former enemy of the Protestant party.

Ronald Formisano, *The Birth of Mass Political Parties, Michigan, 1827-1861,* (Princeton, New Jersey: Princeton Univ. Press, 1971), pp. 44, 295, 330.

[8]HBS, *Old Town Folks,* V. 2, p. 229.

[9]HBS, *Poganuc People,* pp. 68-69.

[10]Introduction to HBS, *Uncle Tom's Emancipation*,
(Philadelphia: Negro History Press, 1853), p. 15.

[11]HBS, *Poganuc People*, p. 234.

[12]Ibid., pp. 164, 84, and *We and Our Neighbors*, p. 146.

[13]HBS, *Pink and White Tyranny*, p. 245.

[14]John Adams remarked in 1790 about flirtatious American
women and wrote a poem describing, "The eye half shut, the
dimpled cheek/ And languid look are cuts too weak/ To win the
heart of any youth/ Who loves simplicity and truth." Page
Smith's explanation of young women's flirtation was the necessity of securing a husband in a society which had lost the
Puritan cohesiveness but retained its freedom in selecting a
mate. (Smith, *Daughters of the Promised Land*, p. 59.)
Henry James was also concerned with American female provoca-
tiveness, as in *Daisy Miller* (1879). Daisy's behavior
scandalized the Romans and the Americans who adopted their
attitudes; she walks arm in arm with two men on the street
and in general does what she pleases. However, in the end,
the narrator, Winterbourne, realizes that she was innocent
and sincere and that he had been too influenced by Europeans
in his loss of respect for her. Lord James Bryce also commented with approval on the free mingling between American
men and women, "the greater measure of freedom in doing what
they will and going where they please...." (Bryce, *The
American Commonwealth*, v. 2, New York: The Commonwealth
Publishing Co., 1908, p. 682. He visited the United States
in 1879, 1881, 1883-84). Stowe did not condemn the association of young men and women either, but rather blamed the
corruption of city life and French manners of flirtation
which tainted the open innocence of American young people.

[15]HBS, *Poganuc People*, p. 124.

[16]William McLoughlin, *The Meaning of Henry Ward Beecher*,
p. 239.

[17]HBS, *Pink and White Tyranny*, p. 186.

[18]HBS, *My Wife and I*, p. 201.

[19]Ibid., p. 96.

[20]J. C. Furnas, *Goodbye to Uncle Tom*, (New York: William
Sloan Associates, 1956), p. 49.

[21]HBS, *Men of Our Times*, p. 117.

[22]Oscar Handlin, *Race and Nationality in American Life*,
(Boston: Little, Brown & Co., 1957), p. 91.

[23]John Higham, *Strangers in the Land*, (New Brunswick,
New Jersey: Rutgers Univ. Press, 1955), p. 10.

[24]Strong was the general secretary of the Evangelical
Alliance, well known for his racist *Our Country*. Strong
concluded that, "Is it not reasonable to believe that this
race is destined to dispossess many weaker ones, assimilate
others, and mould the remainder, until in a very true and
important sense, it has Anglo-Saxonized mankind?" (Sidney
Ahlstrom, *A Religious History of the American People*, New
Haven: Yale Univ. Press, 1972), p. 849.

[25]HBS, *Poganuc People*, p. 226.

[26]HBS, *We and Our Neighbors*, p. 195.

[27]HBS, *Household Papers and Stories*, p. 143.

[28]HBS, *Agnes of Sorrento*, p. 315.

[29]HBS, *The Key to Uncle Tom's Cabin*, (New York: Arno
Press, 1968, first published 1853), p. 402.

[30]His sermons perhaps contributed to the emotional
climate which led to the mob burning of the Ursuline convent
school in Boston.

[31]Winthrop Hudson, *American Protestantism*, (Chicago:
The Univ. of Chicago Press, 1961), p. 88. Presbyterians
shared Lyman's views. The General Assembly of 1835 resolved
to resist Romanism and to attempt to convert its followers
to Biblical truth. They also decided not to accept the
validity of Catholic baptism. The numerous interdenominational voluntary associations were also anti-Catholic. The
Bible society was especially uncompromising, portraying
Catholics as anti-Bible. Societies were formed to specifically combat Popery, such as the American Protestant Association (1842) and the American Protestant Society (1844).

[32]It gained control of the Massachusetts legislature, elected nine governors, eight senators and 104 members of the House of Representatives in 1854.

[33]Gustauvs Myers, *History of Bigotry in the United States*, (New York: Random House, 1943), p. 187.

[34]Billington, *The Protestant Crusade*, p. 412.

[35]Hudson, *American Protestantism*, pp. 110-111.

[36]James Rawley, *Race and Politics*, (New York: J. P. Lippincott, 1969), p. 59.

[37]Charles Stowe, *The Life of Harriet Beecher Stowe*, pp. 157, 202, 16 February 1853 to Mrs. Follen.

[38]Hers was a widespread sentiment. The first issue of the *Liberator* in the 1830s asked "Art thou a parent?" and pictured a slave family on an auction block. See Appendix 2, "A Chronology of HBS' Involvement with the Anti-Slavery Crusade."

[39]Edward Wagenknecht, *Harriet Beecher Stowe: The Known and the Unknown*, (New York: Oxford Univ. Press, 1965), p. 181.

[40]Louis Filler, *The Crusade Against Slavery*, (New York: Harper & Row, 1960), p. 209.

[41]Charles Stowe, *The Life of Harriet Beecher Stowe*, p. 145.

[42]HBS letter to Mrs. Follen, 16 February 1853, quoted in Charles Stowe, *The Life of Harriet Beecher Stowe*, p. 198.

[43]Catharine's stand on abolition elucidated in her letters to Angelina Grimké in 1837 was that women should not participate in politics, they should not even venture to sign petitions to Congress. Rather they should attempt to influence men, as mediators of peace. This policy, she believed, would "most certainly tend to bring to an end, not only slavery, but unnumbered other evils and wrongs." Catharine Beecher, *An Essay on Slavery and Abolitionism in*

Reference to the Duty of American Females, (New York: Books
for Libraries Press, 1970, first published 1837), pp. 128, 146.

[44]HBS used the life of Josiah Hensen as a model for Uncle
Tom and the life of Lewis Clark for George Harris.   She was
also much influenced by the poetry of Frederick Douglas.

[45]HBS wrote an article about Sojourner Truth for the
Atlantic Monthly.

[46]Ryan, "The Cult of Domesticity," p. 335.

[47]She sometimes described "darkies" in terribly racist
terms, such as one, who except for his "intelligent eye, he
might have been taken for a big baboon--the missing link of
Darwin." HBS, *Palmetto Leaves,* p. 269. However, of another
black man, an African, she ascribed no native difference
between him and other men. HBS, *Sunny Memories of Foreign
Lands,* Vol. 2, p. 105.

[48]HBS, *Uncle Tom's Cabin,* (New York: New American
Library, 1966, first published 1863), p. V.

[49]HBS, *Dred,* V. 1, p. 24.

[50]Ibid., V. 2; p. 128, V. 1, p. 198.

[51]Letter from HBS to Douglas (9 July 1851) quoted in
Charles Stowe, *The Life of Harriet Beecher Stowe,* pp. 150-151.

[52]Ibid., p. 265, HBS to Garrison, 18 February 1854.

[53]HBS, *Dred,* V. 2, p. 142.

[54]Ibid., V. 2, pp. 74-75.

[55]Johanna Johnston, *Runaway to Heaven,* (New York:
Doubleday & Co., 1963), p. 47.

[56]Wagenknecht, *Harriet Beecher Stowe,* p. 185.

[57]Ibid., p. 185.

[58]HBS to her family, 4 January 1865, Folder 84,
Schlesinger Archives.

[59]HBS, *Men of Our Times,* p. 110.

CHAPTER SIX

SALVATION APPLIED TO WOMEN

MISOGYNISM

To keep them from competing with men, women were told their place was in the home, for therein they could provide a tranquil haven for men to recuperate from daily responsibilities. One tactic used in keeping women out of professions, politics and ministerial positions was to tell them that their talents were more prominent in feeling than thinking. Science corroborated: according to a study published in 1843, woman had a smaller brain and thus a "natural inferiority of intellect." Woman's power of attention was reported to be feeble. Since she could not focus her thoughts well, she had an "incapacity to distinguish relation, to think in an orderly manner, to generalize...."[1] Even feminist Lucy Stone accepted the theory that smallness meant less power, as witnessed in her belief that women's brains would grow bigger with use. Civil rights leader Soujourner Truth too seemed to accept that men's brains had more capacity, saying "If my cup won't hold but a pint and yours holds a quart, wouldn't ye be mean not to let me have my little half measure fill?"[2] Even the most ardent feminists accepted the theory that women were handicapped by their brain size.[3] Stowe agreed that "woman as a sex ought not to do the hard work of the world, either social, intellectual, or moral. There are evidences in her physiology that this is not intended for her...."[4]

The main focus of female energy was to be found, not in her brain but in her reproductive system and here was her chief value and purpose. If she tried to go against nature and direct too much attention towards learning, dire consequences would result, including sterility, insanity, and ugliness. Directing blood towards the brain does so at the

expense of "the vital organs which are much more important"
to women, and so their "chief value as women is destroyed,"[5]
according to literature of her era. Women as reproductive
agents are propelled more by their instincts and emotions,
are timid and fearful, but are more sympathetic than men.
Any kind of intellectual achievement by a woman was viewed as
threatening. Again and again this same theme is brought
home.

A male character in a magazine story succinctly stated
the prevailing attitude towards the nature of women, saying
to a lady "you admire strength, because you are physically
inferior. You admire intellect, because however intellectual
you may be, you delight still more in the affections." His
lady love was a sweet young girl, dependent on him, and "as
gay as a bird, simple as a child; her own bright nature
investing all things with an ideal halo...."[6] The attractive
woman is one who makes a man feel cheerful, needed and strong.
Man has no desire for more competition in a dog-eat-dog
struggle for economic and personal security.

Respected opinion makers lent weight to the prevailing
ideology. A senator from New Jersey stated in 1866 that
"woman's mission is at home--to assuage the passions of men
as they come in from the battle of life."[7] Adding the legal
stamp to this credo, the Illinois Supreme Court denied women
the right to practice law on the grounds that God has designed
different spheres for men and women. For a woman to appear
in court arguing a case would "destroy the deference and
delicacy with which it is the pride of our ruler sex to treat
her."[8] Thus for women the home came to symbolize the bound-
aries of their lives.

Being intellectual and unattractive went hand in hand,
for the real woman concerned herself with domesticity; only
a plain woman "solaces herself as no young woman ever twice
attempted to do, by reading Plato in solitude."[9] The main

character in a magazine story was carefully taught by her
father, becoming very knowledgeable. The result was the
desiccated fruits of spinsterhood, since her intellectual
attainments were "scarcely calculated to awaken affection"
and she lacked the qualities of a true woman, namely, "the
cheerful song, the merry voice, the bright smile, the buoy-
ant step,"[10] which were pleasing to man.

Even the intellectual Margaret Fuller wrote of woman
as the heart and of man as the head; she believed that woman
was "born for love" and "the cold intellect is ever more
masculine than feminine...."[11] Women who had the advantage
of the best formal education of the time still thought deep
study was ridiculous for women. The writer of the "Shirley
letters" (written in a California mining camp) studied at a
Female Seminary for a year and at Amherst Academy for two
years; yet she believed that "the flower-like delicacy of
the feminine intellect" would be soiled by "pondering over
the wearing stupidities of Presidential elections, or the
bewildering mystifications of rapid metaphysicians." She
believed that woman was characterized by "sweet, shy coque-
tries," not by interest in Kant.[12]

According to Sarah Grimké, women were trained since
childhood to consider marriage their major goal and path to
fulfillment. For girls, marriage was "the only avenue to
distinction," so they concentrated on clothes, dancing, and
other "external charms" in order to attract men.[13] Or, as
another woman explained it, girls were educated for display,
to catch the eye rather than the heart.[14] Women were dressed
like dolls and treated like toys by men. *Godey's* magazine,
whose writers expressed horror at any attempt to take women
from their "empire of home," recognized that women "have too
long been treated like playthings."[15] Other women were seen
as rivals in the race to become married. To be an old maid
was a disaster, and a bright woman was "generally shunned and
regarded as stepping out of her 'appropriate sphere'."[16]

THE CLERGY'S PARTICIPATION

Women were depicted as feeble in mind, body and spirit: physiologically they were smaller than men; theologically they stood in the direct line of inheritance of Eve's guilt and were believed to have sprung from man's rib, almost as a divine afterthought. As one female educator told her students, "As a woman was first in transgression, she should be first in penitence and holiness of character."[17] Another woman educator told girls that they must prove by their piety that the "daughters of Eve could eat at the tree of knowledge... without danger of sin."[18]

St. Paul was quoted to substantiate and justify these social biases, neglecting passages where he praised women leaders in the church (Phoebe, Priscilla, Dorcas) or said that in Christ there was no male or female. He, however, admonished Corinthian women to be silent in church, and sub-mit to the rule of their husbands, for they were the glory of men as men were the glory of Christ, in a kind of descend-ing hierarchy of godliness. An example of the religious inculcation of social attitudes occurred at a children's meeting that the Quaker Sarah Grimké attended, where the question was raised as to the four orders of beings found in the Bible: there are angels, man and beasts; then women, answered one little girl.[19] According to Butler's *The Ameri-can Lady* (1836) a wife, because of her inheritance from Eve, should look to her husband for guidance and "act the more studiously according to his ideas rather than her own." He stated that her duty was to obey her husband, to spread cheerfulness throughout the house, so as to "refresh the faculties of the wise" and to "unbend the brow of the learned." Woman should follow man's superior intellect and soothe him with her greater tenderness and sensitivity. Butler also held that women have a tendency to "unsteadiness of mind" and "repugnancy to grave studies," as well as

"vanity and affectation." Their minds tend, not to steady
reasoning ability but to imagination, "gay vivacity," and
susceptibility to "lively impressions" such as those stirred
up by enthusiastic religion. Because of this unsteadiness
and emotionality, delving into "philosophy and learning are
not the pursuits most improving to the female mind."[20]

The Pastoral Letters of the General Association of
Massachusetts ministers, written in 1837, reveal the same
Pauline themes. The man is the head; woman should aid the
minister with "unostentatious prayers" and lead inquirers to
him. Her domain is the home where man can best defend her
weakness and dependence, given to her by God for her protection. If she involves herself in public reform measures she
presumes the position of a man, so that the ministers warned,
"our care and protection of her seem unnecessary; we put ourselves in self-defense against her, and her character becomes
unnatural." The home is her natural habitat because of her
delicacy and modesty. It is there that her "mild, dependent,
softening influence" can play upon the "sternness of man's
opinions." In an extreme manifestation of such views, a
professor of religion went so far as to direct a pious woman
to worship her husband.[21]

Horace Bushnell, whose work Stowe knew, is another
example of the clergy's participation in the extolling of
women's piety to keep her dependent. In his *Women's Suffrage:
The Reform Against Nature* (1869) he explained that women are
more perceptive and insightful, have a natural piety and
unselfishness, know better how to pray, are finer in their
mold, and have an almost divinely superior ministry. Their
duty is to soothe and civilize men who have been fighting
battles in the outside world and who need women's angelic
influence at home. If they were to leave the seclusion of
their homes to enter into politics and business their very
physiology would change; he threatened women that they would
become bigger, angular, abrupt, lank and lean.

Elizabeth Cady Stanton noted that the prime factor
responsible for women's oppression was not civil law codes
but rather ecclesiastical codes and the male clergy who
interpreted them. They used St. Paul to keep women subordinate to their husbands, silent in public affairs and confined
to the home. From the beginning of American history Puritan
ministers often would not permit a woman to relate her experience of saving grace to her congregation. Rather, they would
tell it for her, not even permitting her to participate in
congregational chanting. They viewed women as sources of
temptation, the sight of whose breasts or backs could kindle
a foul fire in the heart of a male.

The woman's rights movement had to confront Biblical
arguments used to oppose equality for women. After the first
women's rights convention in Seneca Falls in 1848, the *Albany
Register* referred to the participants as "unsexed women, who
make a scoff of religion, who repudiate the Bible and blas-
pheme God...who stalk into the public gaze...."[22] In
response to the convention a local Seneca Falls minister
conducted a series of sermons condemning the woman's rights
movement.

One of the first feminist tracts was written by the
Quaker Sarah Grimké to respond to an 1837 attack by Massachusetts clergy on public reform efforts of women abolitionists. The closing controversial feminist publication of the
century was *The Woman's Bible* organized by Elizabeth Stanton
to liberate women from "bibliotry."

INSPIRED REBELS

Protestant churches provided women with experience in
leadership and organizational skills. Women's church groups
raised money for missionary and charity activities. Women
were the majority of active church workers.

However, women were rarely allowed or encouraged to be
ministers; even by 1901, of 8,000 theology students only
around one hundred were women.[23] Of those who became ministers several were prominent feminists: Antoinette Blackwell
was a leader in the American Women's Suffrage Association
(along with her husband Henry and her closest friend Lucy
Stone) and Universalist minister Anna Howard Shaw was president of the National American Women's Suffrage Association
from 1904 to 1915.

Religion also served as a source of strength for women
when it emphasized the power of mystical grace rather than
doctrinal adherence. Women who believed they were vessels of
inspiration were able to oppose male clergy whom they viewed
as uninspired. A more ambivalent source of strength for
women was the romantic-sentimental-evangelical glorification
of woman's spiritual nature. Both sources were used by HBS
in attacking the clergy and in defense of women's rights.

There is a pattern of strength for women in denominations which emphasize the emotional conversion experience.
Evangelical women participated in Charles Finney's revival
campaign in the Burned-over district of New York. They led
prayer bands, spoke in meetings, and brought their male relatives to the Lord. They "dominated revivals and praying
circles."[24] Mrs. Charles Finney became director of the New
York Female Reform Society and the Methodist Evangelist
Phoebe Palmer helped lead revivals. Neither were feminists
but they certainly did not abide by Pauline dictates to be
silent in public and not to teach men. Examples of later
nineteenth century women evangelists were Methodists Maggie
Van Cott and Amanda Smith who also traveled widely, reaping
souls.

American women who believed they were recipients of
saving grace formed a chain of rebels against the male dominated church establishment. Like Stowe, their passionate

belief in the righteousness of their feelings gave them courage to oppose the clergy. HBS believed, for example, that
Uncle Tom's Cabin was inspired and that she had clearer
understanding of the truth than ministers who opposed her
work to free the slaves.

Quaker women were a vocal component of the anti-slavery
movement and of the woman's rights movement which grew from
abolitionist activities. Quaker abolitionists Sarah and
Angelina Grimké were among the first women to dare to speak
in public despite the fury of New England clergy. In 1837-38
Sarah Grimké replied to the clergy in her *Letters on the
Equality of the Sexes and Condition of Women*. She defined
woman's problems as due to the selfishness of men, including
clergy who monopolize church authority and power. Grimké
explained that clergy mistakenly used St. Paul, who reflected
"Jewish prejudice" about women, to preach that "the greatest
excellence to which a married woman can obtain, is to worship
her husband."

Grimké cited passages in the Bible to justify her conten-
tion that women should have equal rights, including the models
provided by Miriam, Deborah, Huldah, Priscilla and Phoebe.
She reminded her readers that Jesus made no distinction
between male and female virtues and that morality had nothing
to do with being male or female. "All I ask of our brethren,"
she explained, "is that they will take their feet from off
our necks and permit us to stand upright on the ground which
God designed us to occupy."[25]

Other women Quakers prominent in the woman's movement
included minister Lucretia Mott and Susan B. Anthony. Mott
influenced future leader Elizabeth Cady Stanton when the two
were among the American women delegates refused acceptance
at the world's anti-slavery convention held in London in 1840.
Stanton reported later of Mott: "I had never heard a woman
talk of things that, as a Scotch Presbyterian, I had scarcely
dared think."[26]

Stanton grew more and more vocal in her protest against
the clergy. Stanton gathered a committee to comment on the
Bible, encouraged by the climate of higher criticism of the
Bible introduced to America in the 80s and 90s and the
movement against literal interpretation of the Bible.

Part one of *The Woman's Bible* was published in 1895, on
the Pentateuch, and part two, on the rest of the Bible, was
published in 1898. A storm of protests occurred indicting
Stanton's project as the work of the devil. She replied,
"This is a grave mistake. His Satanic majesty was not
invited to join the Revising Committee, which consists of
women alone."[27] In 1896 even the National American Woman's
Suffrage Association disavowed *The Woman's Bible*; future
presidents Carrie Chapman Catt and Anna Howard Shaw voted
with the majority. The debate over Stanton's bible was a
decisive move away from radicalism toward practical political tactics aimed at gaining suffrage and toward social
feminism's acceptance of Victorian values. These values were
both the impetus for the woman's movement and the source of
its failure to gain equal power for women in church and
society.

VICTORIAN FEMINISM

By adopting the Victorian notion of a lady and the moral
superiority tack, feminists accepted restriction of women to
a limited sphere of social service. They also denied their
sexuality by viewing sex as men's lesser realm. For example,
Victorian feminists opposed birth control on the grounds that
it encouraged men's lustful desires. Also, the notion of
different spheres separated women from men and emphasized the
sorority of pure women apart from immoral bestial men.
Around sixty to seventy percent of the first generation of
graduates from women's colleges did not marry.[28]

The Declaration of Sentiments issued by the Seneca
Falls Convention in 1848 attempted to make use of the moral

superiority argument to justify women's suffrage and public
speaking. Composed mainly by Stanton with ideas contributed
by Anthony, the Declaration resolved that

> Inasmuch as man, while claiming for himself intel-
> lectual superiority, does accord to woman moral
> superiority, it is preeminently his duty to
> encourage her to speak and teach, as she has an
> opportunity, in all religious assemblies.

But, aiming to eradicate the double standard of virtue, they
resolved that

> the same amount of virtue, delicacy and refinement
> of behavior that is required of women in the
> social state, should also be required of man, and
> the same transgression should be visited with
> equal severity on both man and woman.[29]

However, partly because of Stanton's advocacy of freer
divorce laws and her support of radical Victoria Woodhull,
the Women's Suffrage Association split in 1869 into the NWSA,
National Woman's Suffrage Association (Stanton, Anthony, New
York based) and the AMSA, American Women's Suffrage Association (Stone, Blackwells, Julia Howe, Boston based). The
most publicized reason for the split was controversy over
support of black male suffrage and the Fourteenth Amendment
as the Boston group was for it and the New York group for
women's rights above all else.

After the Woodhull scandal in the 1870s caused by her
declaration of free love and accusations that Henry Ward
Beecher practiced the same ethic, feminists less brave than
Stanton no longer challenged the ideals of Victorian marriage. The post-Civil War Gilded Age was a conservative
era, its reform energies having been spent in fighting the
Civil War. The 1870s saw the expansion of moral purity
movements, the Comstock law which banned the sale or dispensing of contraception through the mails, and even the
popular HBS received devastating attacks for her publication
of the alleged details of Lord Byron's illicit sexual

activities. By the time of the reunion of the NAWSA in 1890,
criticism of the marriage system stood mute.

Most feminists succumbed and used the values associated
with Victorian marriage to justify the woman's movement.
After Stanton and Anthony died the second generation of
social feminists, including Carrie Chapman Catt, Anna Howard
Shaw, and Harriet Stanton Blatch, used the same argument
which Stowe preached that the state was a larger family which
needed woman's influence in education, temperance, slum
clearance and other reform movements. Jane Adams explained
in 1878 that the "state is but the larger family...and that
in this national home there is room and a corner and a duty
for mother."[30] This was precisely the view that HBS did so
much to popularize. Social feminists campaigned for equality
not on the basis of equal rights as human beings but on the
basis of their virtue as mothers. When women's suffrage was
finally granted it did not result in great moral changes and
that made the social feminist argument seem absurd. The
deference granted to women by chivalrous men had succeeded
in keeping women from militancy.

THE BEECHERS ON THE WOMEN'S MOVEMENT

The Beechers took very different positions from each
other on the woman's movement. Catharine took a strong
stand against suffrage, believing that women could get what
they wanted without the ballot, that it would create rivalry
between the sexes, and that woman's role was as priestess of
her home or schoolroom. She did not believe in the automatic
transfer of emotion to righteous action, without reasonable
deliberation. She was critical of the women's rights leaders
saying that "A large proportion of those who demand woman
suffrage are persons who have not been trained to reason,
and are chiefly guided by their generous sensibilities."[31]
Henry Ward Beecher served as President of the American Woman's

Suffrage Association, which was more conservative than the
National Women's Suffrage Association.

Isabella Beecher Hooker (d. 1907) was the most flamboy-
ant Beecher supporter of the woman's movement. Together with
her lawyer husband she studied Blackstone on the paucity of
legal rights for women. Hooker succeeded in his sponsorship
of a bill to provide legal rights for married women in
Connecticut, passed in 1871, after seven years of advocacy.
Isabella helped to found the New England Suffrage Association,
engaged in speaking tours, addressed the Judiciary Committee
of the U. S. Senate, and wrote two tracts on women. She
became a Victoria Woodhull supporter, joining in her involvement in spiritualism. Isabella received a spirit message
that a matriarchy, headed by herself, would usher in the
millenium. Furthermore, she believed Woodhull's accusation
rather than Henry Ward's denial of adultery, alienating
members of her family, including Harriet who acted as guard
to make sure that Isabella did not try to speak in Henry's
Brooklyn church.

Although Stowe did so much to foment public opinion
against slavery, she accepted the Victorian notion of their
being limitations in women's intellect. This meant that
they were limited to the sheltered world of their homes.
HBS echoed the prevalent views of her age, including the
gilding of woman's cage by the rhetoric that told woman she
was more moral, pure, and spiritual than her captors. HBS
accepted the confinement of woman to her pedestal.

Stowe was a disappointment to the feminists who felt
that she was afraid to take a strong stand. However, one of
her biographers called Stowe's *Lady Byron Vindicated* a
feminist tract, a rebellion against men which was caused by
her resentment of the lack of attention from her father and
husband.[32] In it she criticized English law and custom as
unjust to women. She pointed out that Lady Byron had a

deeper mind than her husband; if she had been born a man she
might have guided English thought. Many women like Lady
Byron were the helpless victims of male cruelties, she
observed.

HBS was reserved, however, in her advocacy of the woman's
movement. Her emphasis was always on woman's home duties to
her family. She believed that women's rights advocates had
"not sufficiently considered the propriety of straightening,
widening, and mending the good old house and home."[33] For
example, one of her characters was an Irish woman who endured
her basically good but occasionally drunk husband; HBS
believed she was "a revelation of the Christ-like spirit a
thousand times more than if she was tramping to a Women's
Rights convention."[34] Another female character was independent, strong, and a teacher of classical languages; HBS
described her as like Sojourner Truth in that she took action
without any "fol-de-rol about Women's Rights."[35] She
jokingly suggested that the way to end women's inequality
was to go on strike by not taking care of the babies until
the laws were altered; one week, she said, would bring the
men around.

Stowe was critical of two kinds of feminists, those who
attacked traditional roles and those who used feeling or
spiritualism to deduce that women were superior: the second
shows Catharine's influence because HBS' proclivity was to
do just that. An example of the first kind of bad woman is
her character Audacia Dangyereyes, a parody of Victoria
Woodhull. She drinks, smokes, addresses men as "bub," and
invites them to call on her in her room, telling them to
look upon her as just "another fellow."[36] An example of the
second is Mrs. Stella Cerulean, who thought everything ought
to be based on love and instinct. Through her supposedly
"divine intuitions of womanhood" and spiritualistic communications she concluded that women were superior. She looked

for a future time when women could do whatever they please,
including putting an end to a marriage relation.[37] Stowe
granted, however, that the majority of women's rights leaders
were "true and noble women, and worthy of all the reverence
due to such."[38]

Stowe had one of her capable, bright, self-sufficient
women conclude that suffrage should not be granted to women
until they had more education and "better balanced minds."[39]
HBS warned through another character that politics was so
wicked that only a "brazen tramp" could enter into it, and
that if women did get involved in political power processes
it would destroy "the delicacy and refinement of feeling
which...American men especially, cherish toward women."[40]
She explained that women could not afford to lose the good
will of men since women were weaker and not as capable of
self-support. (The Massachusetts clergy who so outraged
Sarah Grimké had used the same arguments against women's
involvement in the world outside the home.)

Having warned women of their dependency on men and the
vileness of politics, Stowe did advocate the vote for women
on the basis of the social feminists' theme of the nation as
an extended family. The only way to save the nation from
corruption was to give women the vote, especially in regards
to education, temperance, morals and religion. She noted
that, "All places where women are excluded tend downward to
barbarism; but the moment she is introduced, there comes in
with her courtesy, cleanliness, sobriety, and order." She
believed in the necessity of "State housekeeping" by women,
for until they vote and have an equal voice with men a perfect State cannot exist, as she defined it.[41] She justified
the propriety of women speaking in public by stating that
speech making is no more public than dancing at a huge ball.
Besides, women always end up ruling men anyway, through their
"jawin', kissin' and faculty" (the last term refers to their

managerial abilities). They are "in some way the first or
the last cause of everything that is going on."[42] But their
main avenue of influence was an indirect one through the
home, not the rude political arena, at least until their
influence refined it.

She also defended the intellectual ability of women.
She portrayed many of her young female characters as bright
and capable scholars. Mara (*Pearl*) is better than Moses at
learning Latin. Tina (*OTF*) would have been capable of doing
as well at Harvard as her male friends. Stowe added that a
classroom of all males is cloddish and lumpish; it needs the
presence of women to add sparkle and thoroughness in point
of view. Minerva Randall (*OTF*) knew Greek, Latin and mathe-
matics and navigated a ship home when her brother became
ill. However, like all of Stowe's intellectual women, she
is unmarried; somehow intellect and heart could not coexist
in a woman, in Stowe's eyes.

Women should be free to pursue professional studies and
careers, especially self-sufficient women who feel no need
for husband and children. Her character Ida (*Wife*), a
spinster, went off to study in England, "fitting herself to
make new and better paths for women."[43] She also praised
physical strength in women like her spunky heroine who could
lift a barrel of flour unaided.

Through her own experience HBS recognized that the
drudgery of married life and constant concern with puddings
and shirt buttons could sap the "sparkle and vivacity" of a
young bride. She also voiced the jealousy of girls like
herself who envied the freedom of their brothers who could
grow up and patriotically fight for their country and perhaps "do something glorious like General Washington."
Women should not be left with all the child care; their husbands should help stay up at night with sick babies, etc.
Neighborhood laundries and bakeries and cook shops would be

less work than each family doing its own, an argument used
later by her great niece, feminist Charlotte Perkins Gilman.
The emphasis on dress also threatened to smother women and
waste their energies, she realized.

Stowe recognized that women had been left out of his-
tories such as Plutarch's *Lives*, that woman was "too often a
sufferer" and the recipient of "the unjust and unequal
burdens."[44] She saw women's rights advocates as preparing
the way for future good. The state, as well as the home,
needed women's spirituality.

HBS as a Protestant crusader felt the need to reform
society. The most blatant violator of family life and women's
purity was slavery. When she had successfully fought that
battle she next fought for women abused by city life, urging
them to create havens of beauty and spirituality in their
homes. She did not give much time to the women's rights
movement because she believed that women are too pure and
delicate to compete with men for political or economic power.
Like social feminists she urged women to expand their mother-
ing qualities to a wider sphere than their homes; for that
reason she advocated women's right to vote.

By defining women as more pious, less sexual and less
selfish, however, she denied them the rights that belong to
all human beings because they are human and not merely
because they are pious. She did much to help free black
slaves but she also did much to shackle women to domesticity
and the avoidance of competition with men. Such roles
clearly impeded the achievement of equal rights for women.

NOTES

[1]Alexander Walker, *Woman Physiologically Considered*,
(New York: Langly, 1845), p. 56.

[2]Francis Titus, *Narrative of Sojourner Truth*, (New York:
Arno Press, 1968; first published 1878), p. 134.

[3]However, in her book *The Sexes Throughout Nature* (1875)
Antoinette Brown Blackwell critically quoted evolutionists
Darwin and Spencer as placing women's intellect on a scale
intermediate between men and children, just as their bodies
and brains are intermediate in size.

[4]HBS, *House and Home Papers*, p. 306.

[5]Walker, *Women Physiologically Considered*, pp. 58-59.

[6]Mrs. Smith, "The Bud and the Blossom," *Graham's Magazine*, V. XXI, No. 2 (August 1842), p. 62.

[7]Eleanor Flexnor, *Century of Struggle*, (New York:
Atheneum, 1972), p. 148.

[8]Ibid., p. 121.

[9]"How John Wolfe Got His Rich Wife," *Putnam's Magazine*,
V. 1, No. 6 (December 1857), p. 731.

[10]Mrs. Emma Einbury, "The Brother and The Sister,"
Graham's Magazine, V. XXI, No. 1 (July 1842), p. 41.

[11]Fuller, *Woman in The Nineteenth Century*, p. 103.

[12]Louise Clappe, *The Shirley Letters*, (Santa Barbara:
Peregrine, 1970), p. 80.

[13]Grimké, *Letters on the Equality of the Sexes*, p. 11.

[14]*Graham's Magazine*, V. XXI, No. 6 (December 1842),
p. 336.

[15]Riegel, *American Women*, p. 25.

[16]Grimké, *Letters on the Equality of the Sexes*, p. 46.

[17]Riegel, *American Women*, p. 36.

[18]*Ibid.*, p. 64.

[19]Grimké, *Letters on the Equality of the Sexes*, p. 64.

[20]Butler, *The American Lady*, pp. 219, 21, 27, 218.

[21]Grimké, *Letters on the Equality of the Sexes*, pp. 18, 20, 11, 90.

[22]Smith, *Daughters of the Promised Land*, p. 120.

[23]Riegel, *American Women*, p. 185. When women did assume leadership positions it was often connected with freedom from domesticity, either through widowhood, spinsterhood, or monastic life such as produced Catholic abbesses and sainted mystics.

[24]Whitney Cross, *The Burned-over District*, (Ithaca: Cornell Univ. Press, 1950), p. 177. Another product of the Burned-over area was feminist, reformer, and first woman ordained Congregational minister, Antoinette Brown Blackwell. Also, western New York was the site of the first women's rights convention.

[25]Grimké, *Letters on the Equality of the Sexes*, p. 90, for preceding quotation, p. 10.

[26]Smith, *Daughters of the Promised Land*, p. 109.

[27]Aileen Kraditor, *The Ideas of the Woman Suffrage Movement, 1890-1920*, (New York: Doubleday, 1971), p. 67.

[28]Jill Conway, "Perspectives on Women's Education in the United States," *History of Education Quarterly*, V. XIV, No. 1, Spring 1974), p. 8.

[29]*Ms. Magazine*, V. 1, No. 13, July 1973, p. 46.

[30]Freedman and Shade, *Our American Sisters*, p. 305.

[31]Parker, *The Oven Birds*, p. 28.

[32]Rourke, *Trumpets of Jubilee*, p. 142.

[33]HBS, *Household Papers*, p. 246.

[34]HBS, *My Wife and I*, p. 289.

[35]HBS, *Old Town Folks*, V. 2, p. 40.

[36]HBS, *My Wife and I*, pp. 251-252.

[37]Ibid., p. 244.

[38]HBS, *Household Papers*, p. 245.

[39]HBS, *My Wife and I*, p. 272.

[40]HBS, *Household Papers*, p. 270.

[41]Ibid., p. 252.

[42]HBS, *Old Town Folks*, V. 2, p. 8.

[43]HBS, *My Wife and I*, p. 222.

[44]HBS, *Household Papers*, p. 139.

CHAPTER SEVEN

THE LEGACY

Harriet Beecher Stowe was one of the most widely read novelists of the nineteenth century. The passions and concerns which she felt were shared by her contemporaries. Colonial society had been mainly composed of people who shared common ties with English culture, religion and government. This relative homogeneity was diluted in the nineteenth century by the massive influx of immigrants into growing industrial areas. Developments in science gave rise to questions about Biblical teachings. The rigid intellectual discipline demanded by New England clergy was loosened by revivals with a western tone. Like HBS, Americans were concerned about the divisions and disruptions brought about by denominational quarrels, sectional rivalry and industrialization. Stowe voiced common fears and provided a solution.

Her response to the problems of slavery, of theology in a new age, and of city life was to strengthen home and family. This was one arena where the individual could exert some influence. She taught women how to create a saving, peaceful environment in their homes; how to charmingly inspire men; how to decorate their clothes, their walls and furniture in an inexpensive but lovely manner; and how to expand the home sanctuary to friends and neighbors in quiet fireside dinners and conversations. Her defense of beauty, of art and decoration suited the mood of a more affluent century. She also expressed nostalgia for the tranquility and homogeneity of the New England past, proclaiming its virtues and chiding its religious errors.

Harriet Beecher Stowe reacted against male clergy who gave their attention to theological disputes about definitional issues of minor import, who preached both free will

and inability not to sin, and who moved against dancing
rather than slavery. Instead of the New England reliance on
"metaphysical algebra" she used the sentiment of Romantic
philosophers and sentimental novelists to find understanding
in the heart rather than in the intellect. Women like Stowe
attacked theological formulas; in so doing they began to
awaken "the heathenized churches out of their hideous dream,"
as Oliver Wendell Holmes observed.[1] In the process Stowe
held up women as the prime model of proper piety.

Her brother Henry also preached the heart gospel of the
importance of love, as did other liberal Protestant clergy.
Like her, he spoke of "the dreadful way in which the old
theology represented God--burning with wrath--scorching,
scathing so that the sinner could not get at his feelings or
his heart without some arrangements and machinery to get him
right," as HBS explained it.[2]

Stowe popularized in her novels the theme developed by
her sister Catharine that self-sacrificing women were the
most effective vehicles used by Christ for salvation. HBS
taught that one cannot understand Christ "till you have loved
somebody better than yourselves.... God has no self--but lives
in the happiness of others."[3] Her description of God sounds
much like her definition of a good woman. This definition
gave women some status in spirituality while they were
denied access to economic and political power, and to church
leadership. It was convenient for men to hand religious and
moral responsibility to their mothers and wives; as St. Clare
explained in *Uncle Tom's Cabin*, "Your piety sheds respectability on us."[4] The little girl who wore a boy's black coat
to try to meet her father's wish that she was a boy, wielded
influence with her novels about the spiritual power of women.
Her attempt, however, to carve out an important role for
women in religion was based on a glorification of their
purity which served to relegate them to their homes, away
from the rough and tumble of life in the marketplace.

Stowe reflected her contemporaries' idealization of
women as a substitute for religious certainty and for religious piety. However, there is a passive quality in the
heroines of magazine articles and novels who find their
identity in pleasing their husband and children. HBS was
different in her emphasis on women as initiators, savers of
the souls they attracted to their church-like homes. The
innovator of this activist stance was probably Catharine
Beecher, who as a single woman, could not find her purpose
in a family and instead encouraged the Christian civilizing
role of women as teachers and nurses as well as the prime
ministers of their homes (career and domesticity were not
to be simultaneous). It is true that some of HBS' heroines'
redeeming impact is in the ultimate act of passivity--their
resigned deaths (i.e., Eva in *UTC* (1852) and Mara in *Pearl*
(1862)). But in *My Wife and I* (1871), for example, the
heroine consciously draws in friends and neighbors to her
home-church and provides salvation for Molly, St. John, etc.
Dolly preaches to and saves Zeph in *Poganuc People* (1878).
HBS added to popular literature a dimension of leadership
and initiative that was often missing in her early short
stories and the fictional works of other authors who glorified women's spirituality.

Stowe, then, is like other nineteenth century authors
who portrayed women as angelic, innocent, pure, and beautiful, serving to give men anchors, to provide stable peaceful
homes for men and children. She is innovative in that she
builds on the common notion of women's purity to maintain
that men require a pious mother, sister or wife in order to
be saved. All of her male characters have women as their
vehicles of grace, none are saved by clergy. Stowe noted
that there are only two aids to salvation: "One is God, and
the other is a true, good woman. God you will have, but the
woman--she must be found."[5] She observed that most good

boys who grow into good men do so because they have "unlim-
ited faith in women."[6] She would never make the reverse
statement for women. In summation, "the love of woman is a
religion! a baptism! a consecration!"[7]

Women were aided in their salvation by love and marriage, as was Nina (Dred), Lille (PWT) and Esther (OTF) but,
unlike men, some women had the necessary refinement and
insight to obtain grace on their own without the influence
of the opposite sex: Mary (MW), Mara (Pearl) and Dolly (PP).
"The purer truth of spiritual instruction" is more available
to women than to men.[8] Women have "the divine gift of prophecy" because of their nature as women--humble, less sexual,
more intuitive.[9] Due to their tender hearts, they were most
damaged by male New England theology; women "found it hard-
est to tolerate it or to assimilate it, and many a delicate
and sensitive nature was utterly wrecked in the struggle,"
as HBS felt about her own struggles with theology.[10]

It is apparent that the central theme of Stowe's novels
is the redemptive power of refined womanhood, yet none of
the Stowe scholars developed her main purpose prior to 1977.
The one to do so with the most attention was Alice Crozier,
but she did not do so systematically. Instead she stressed
Stowe's concern to provide an ordered existence in an urban
setting. This theme was important to HBS in her three
novels with a New York setting but her consistent purpose
in each novel she wrote was to preach the primacy of women
as vehicles of earthly grace. Others noted the importance
of her heroines only in passing. I believe that the reason
for the neglect of her glorification of women's spirituality
is that women have had little power or status in our society
and are therefore not an important subject to which to give
scholarly attention. Why else has the major and obviously
overriding theme of the most popular nineteenth century
novelist been ignored?

The legacy of this praise of women was disastrous for
twentieth century women. Disillusionment with the motherly
angelic woman as a panacea for societal ills occurred in the
late nineteenth century when it became apparent that problems were not being resolved by family nurture. Later it
was recognized that women's voting patterns could not be
distinguished from men's. Women had made the mistake of
asking for their civil rights, not on the grounds of equal
adulthood, but on the basis of moral superiority. Like HBS,
they argued that mother-power could reform America, clean
up her slums, put an end to alcohol addiction, and improve
labor conditions, especially for children. But when women
received suffrage they joined with men to elect President
Harding, maker of bathtub gin in the White House and the
source of political scandal. The fall of woman from her
pedestal that resulted partially from the failure of women's
vote or their advocacy of prohibition to make society better
was reflected in the novels of the 1920s. They show the
historical swing of the pendulum from woman as angel to
temptress and source of trouble, like Fitzgerald's Daisy
Buchanan in *The Great Gatsby*, although Daisy too is a victim
of American society.

Another trend in the twentieth century is the continua-
tion of Stowe's theme of woman as heart, male as brain. The
two most popular women leaders in religion abided by male
definitions of woman's powers. Sister Aimee McPhersen (1890-
1944) knew that she was "only a girl," but felt that God
could use even her as a vessel, a mouthpiece, and a channel
for His work. She always dressed in white. She defined
herself as operating out of a mother heart as a "little
mother evangelist" preaching love and joy rather than the
"mazes of man's theology."[11] Kathryn Kuhlman (c. 1907-1976)
said that she was "all woman." She did not form a church
for she believed that kind of authority and leadership

belongs to men. She also appeared to her vast audiences
dressed in a white gown of purity. Kuhlman and McPhersen
continued Stowe's identification of women as oriented to
the heart rather than the mind and closely tied to the role
of nurturing mother.

The theme of women's affinity with emotions continued
and flowered in the 1950s. Even liberal thinkers like
Adlai Stevenson accepted the "Feminine Mystique," telling
the American Woman in 1955 that her role was to "inspire in
her home a vision of the meaning of life and freedom...to
help her husband find values that will give purpose to his
specialized daily chores...to teach her children the unique-
ness of each individual human being."[12] The stereotypic
ideas of woman's nurturant and loving sentiments are still
celebrated. Gallantry and romanticism are tools used by the
society to keep women focusing their energy on men, as
explained by Shulamith Firestone. Women are still taught
that love fills their needs. To attract a husband they are
required to fit the culture's definition of a valuable woman
so that "Love, perhaps even more than childbearing, is the
pivot of women's oppression today."[13] Stowe reinforced the
language of romantic love.

Twentieth century feminists have turned away from what
Charlotte Perkins Gilman identified as modern "motherolatry":
she attacked the contemporary notions of motherhood in her
Women and Economics (1898). As a transitional figure Gilman
continued much of the emphasis on motherhood as causing women
to be altruistic, loving and concerned with social progress.
She explained that, "the desire of the mother soul is to
give benefit rather than to receive it." Women see the word
"life" not as a noun but as "living", an active verb.[14]
Gilman advocated that alert mothers who carefully selected
their mates could "send forth a new kind of people to help
the world...," instead of being used as servants and

pseudo-mothers to their husbands. She hoped for the "mother
who is uprising, whose deep, sweet current of uplifting love
is to pour forward into service." She saw motherhood as the
"supreme power of the world...."[15]

In opposition are male values which Gilman believed
stemmed from men's original role as hunters, projecting a
God of violence, wrath, vengefulness, pride and judgment.
Male religion stresses obedience and submission. Like HBS,
she faulted Calvinism and the notion of being willing to be
damned for God's glory as faulty male logic.[16]

Current feminist theologians still touch on the theme
of motherhood. Women from Stowe to Mary Daly have searched
for historical models and images. They focus on the Virgin
Mary as one of the few feminine symbols in Christianity.
The Virgin must be symbolically free and "save" the Son,
writes Daly. But while the Virgin was important only in her
relationship to her Son, "The New Being of antichurch is a
rising up of Mother and Daughter together, beyond the
Madonna's image and beyond the ambivalent Warrior-Maiden's
self-image [of Joan of Arc]."[17]

From the second wave of the woman's movement in the
1960s emerged feminist theologians who are attempting to
struggle as HBS did to find a place for women in the churches
but without resorting to utilization of male projections of
unwanted ideals on women. The dearth of women in leadership
roles in the church is still omnipresent; churches have
generally resisted according women equal rights.

HBS used the traits of loving self-sacrifice projected
on women by men to try to develop a sense of worth for subordinate women. Her strategy of giving pious women responsibility for converting souls was not realistic. Twentieth
century feminist theologians are still attempting to solve
the problem of women's low status in the church. Some perhaps continue to make the same error of exalting women as

different from men in a female egalitarian cooperative
spirit--which may only be a result of being oppressed.   HBS'
works embodied the popular thought of her era and both
reflected and shaped attitudes toward the religious roles of
women.

Notes

[1]McCray, *The Life-Work of the Author of Uncle Tom's Cabin*, p. 255.

[2]HBS to the twins, 8 March 1859, Brooklyn, Folder 103, Schlesinger Archives.

[3]Ibid.

[4]HBS, *Uncle Tom's Cabin*, p. 199.

[5]HBS, *My Wife and I*, pp. 97-98.

[6]HBS, *Pink and White Tyranny*, p. 60.

[7]HBS, *Old Town Folks*, V. 2, p. 86.

[8]HBS, *The Pearl of Orr's Island*, p. 163.

[9]HBS, *House and Home Papers*, p. 245.

[10]HBS, *Old Town Folks*, V. 2, p. 55.

[11]Aimee Temple McPhersen, *In the Service of the King: The Story of My Life*, (New York: Boni and Liverwright, 1927), p. 89.

[12]Betty Friedan, *The Feminine Mystique*, (New York: Bell Publishing Co., 1963), p. 40.

[13]Shulamith Firestone, *The Dialectic of Sex: The Case for Feminist Revolution*, (New York: Bantam Books, 1970), see chapter six on "Love."

[14]A major theme of the feminist theologian Mary Daly, of a later generation. See *Beyond God the Father: Toward a Philosophy of Woman's Liberation*, (Boston: Beacon Press, 1973.

[15]Charlotte Perkins Gilman, *His Religion and Hers: A Study of Our Fathers and the Work of Our Mothers*, (New York and London: The Century Co., 1923), pp. 92, 277, 279, 294.

[16]Ibid., p. 160.

[17]Daly, *Beyond God the Father: Toward a Philosophy of Woman's Liberation*, p. 150.

SELECTED BIBLIOGRAPHICAL SOURCES
HARRIET BEECHER STOWE, AN ANNOTATED BIBLIOGRAPHY OF PRIMARY AND SECONDARY SOURCES

MANUSCRIPT SOURCES

Radcliffe's Schlesinger Library, Cambridge, Mass., Women in America archives. This is the richest source of HBS letters to her family.

Huntington Library, Los Angeles, Calif. It owns nearly 200 HBS letters and about twenty letters written by her husband. (Her letters are mainly to Mr. and Mrs. Fields.)

HBS' PUBLISHED WORKS (Listed in order of publication)

Thirty books, including a geography text, children's stories, religious poems and sketches, biographies, a book on the Byron controversy, travel letters, collections of short stories, articles on homemaking, and ten novels. She also wrote numerous articles for newspapers such as *The Evangelist, National Era, Godey's Lady's Book, Independent,* and the *Christian Union.*

The Mayflower. New York: Harper & Bros., 1843. A collection of HBS' earliest short stories, revolving around New England.

Stories, Sketches and Studies, The Writings of Harriet Beecher Stowe, Vol. XIV. Cambridge, Mass.: Houghton, Mifflin, 1896.

Edmonson Family and the Capture of the Schooner Pearl. Cincinnati, Ohio: American Reform Tract & Book Society, 1850. About the evils of slavery for children who are taken from their parents and forbidden to pray.

The Two Altars; or, Two Pictures as One. New York: Anti-Slavery Society, Tract #13, 1852. The story of a freed slave who does well in the North, but is recaptured "a bleeding wreck on the altar of liberty."

Uncle Tom's Cabin. New York: New American Library, 1966; first published in 1853. Uncle Tom is sold, shares the love of Christ with Little Eva, whose death converts family members. Tom is sold again, to terrible Simon Legree. Eliza and George escape from Tom's original master, Shelby, and reach Canada after various adventures.

The Key to Uncle Tom's Cabin. New York: Arno Press, 1968;
first published in 1853. A collection of data to prove
Uncle Tom's Cabin factual. Includes copies of court
cases, advertisements for fugitive slaves, etc.

Sunny Memories of Foreign Lands. 2 Vols. Boston: Phillips,
Sampson & Co., 1854. A collection of letters written
from Europe in 1853. Includes comments on Scotch
Calvinism and on Roman Catholicism.

Dred: A Tale of the Great Dismal Swamp. 2 Vols. New York:
AMS Press, Inc., 1967, V. 344 but first published in
1856. Dred is a black outlaw in the swamps of North
Carolina. The degradation of poor whites is shown as
is the futility of the just white plantation owner,
Clayton, who aims to free his slaves. A subplot
centers around the spiritualizing love affair of Clayton
and Nina.

The Minister's Wooing. New York: Derby and Jackson, 1859.
Takes place in Newport, Rhode Island in the late eighteenth century. Mary Scudder falls in love with James
Marvyn. He is believed lost at sea as a sailor.
Dr. Hopkins, minister and boarder at the Scudder home,
proposes marriage to Mary. She accepts. James returns
unexpectedly. Dr. Hopkins releases her from her promise, acting on "disinterested benevolence." A subplot involves Aaron Burr's attempt to seduce a married
French woman.

Agnes of Sorrento. New York: AMS Press, Inc., 1967, V. 7;
first published in 1862. Takes place in fifteenth century Italy. Agnes is a young peasant who falls in love
with a noble outlaw, Agostino. Her confessor tries to
direct her toward the convent. She discovers her
father was a noble, realizes the beauties of the world,
marries Agostino.

The Pearl of Orr's Island. New York: AMS Press, Inc., 1967,
V. 6; first published in 1862. Moses is shipwrecked as
an infant, is taken in by a Maine family. He falls in
love with the daughter, Mara. Her untimely death saves
his soul and their friend Sally. Moses and Sally marry.

Household Papers and Stories. New York: AMS Press, Inc.,
1967, V. 8; first published in the 1860s in a series
in *The Atlantic Monthly.* A collection of stories about
problems and solutions in the domestic household of the
commentator. Includes advice about decorating homes,
managing servants, women's rights.

Religious Studies and Poems. New York: AMS Press, Inc.,
1967, V. 15; first published as *Religious Poems* in
1867 and *Footsteps of the Master* in 1877.

Men of Our Times. Hartford, Conn.: Hartford Publishers Co.,
1868. Biographies of statesmen mostly connected with
the Civil War. A valuable chapter on Henry Ward Beecher.

Lady Byron Vindicated. New York: Haskell House, 1970; first
published in 1870. An account of marriage to Lady Byron,
his love affair with his stepsister, his ill treatment
of his wife. Comments on the injustice of English law
to women.

Old Town Folks. 2 Vols. New York: AMS Press, Inc., 1967,
V. 9-10; first published in 1869. Based on Calvin
Stowe's youth in Natich, Massachusetts. Calvin is por-
trayed as the visionary Horace who eventually married
Tina, after her lesson of suffering married to Ellery
Davenport, grandson of Jonathan Edwards. Horace's
friend Harry marries Esther; they are Episcopalians,
saving Esther from her inability to duplicate the con-
version experience required by her minister father,
Mr. Avery (who is like Lyman Beecher).

Old Town Fireside Stories. New York: AMS Press, Inc., 1966,
Vol. 11; first published in 1871. A collection of
stories about Sam Lawson, a favorite character from
Old Town Folks.

Pink and White Tyranny. Boston: Roberts Brothers, 1871.
A New York society novel. Lilly is a spoiled beautiful
girl who marries for financial security. Her true love
returns after a long absence. She flirts with him and
is sinful in many other ways. She is saved by her suffering during an illness and by her husband's compassion.

My Wife and I. New York: AMS Press, Inc., 1967, V. 12;
first published in 1871. Set in New York City during
the Gilded Age. Harry and Eva are married, their home
serves as a shrine of comfort to neighbors and friends.
They plan to modify the ascetic life of the Episcopal
priest, St. John, who marries Eva's sister.

Palmetto Leaves. Gainesville, Florida: University of
Florida Press, 1968; first published in 1873. A
description of the beauties of nature in Florida.
Comments on freedmen.

We and Our Neighbors. New York: AMS Press, Inc., 1967, V. 13;
first published in 1875. The sequel to *My Wife and I*
in which various friends are matched in marriage.

Poganuc People. New York: AMS Press, Inc., 1967, Vol. 11;
    first published in 1878. A semi-autobiographical novel
    set in New England during the struggle for religious
    toleration in Connecticut. Dolly (Harriet's view of
    herself) is drawn to the Episcopal Church, despite her
    clergyman father's strict Calvinism, and eventually
    joins the Episcopal Church to marry a young wealthy
    Englishman and sends her son to Harvard.

AN ANNOTATED BIBLIOGRAPHY OF WORKS BY STOWE SCHOLARS

The standard biographies are Annie Fields, 1898; Charles Stowe,
    1891; Charles and Lyman Stowe, 1911; Lyman Stowe, 1934;
    and Forrest Wilson, 1941.

Adams, John. *Harriet Beecher Stowe.* New York: Twayne Pub-
    lishers, 1963. HBS reacts to her childhood subservience
    to Lyman and Catharine; she identifies with slaves. She
    opposes her father's "religion of law" with her "reli-
    gion of love." She teaches the moral superiority of
    women.

Cross, Barbara, ed., *Autobiography of Lyman Beecher,* 2 Vols.
    Cambridge, Mass.: Belknap Press, 1961. Around 1850
    Lyman began his autobiography. Six of his children took
    notes. They also collected letters and some added their
    own recollections. Charles arranged the material and
    it was published in 1864. Themes which influenced HBS:
    1) "the importance of Roxanna, a Saint"; 2) "the power
    of the heart set on fire by love is the greatest created
    power in the universe"; 3) pragmatic revivalism, to save
    souls, make changes in theological statements, or to
    save a sheep, make changes in the fold.

Crozier, Alice. *The Novels of Harriet Beecher Stowe.* New
    York: Oxford Univ. Press, 1969. HBS blames Jonathan
    Edwards' rationalism for perverting the true Puritan
    way. Before the Civil War HBS taught evangelical sal-
    vation, as best preached by mothers and angelic virginal
    heroines. After the war she turned away from theology
    to sentimental aesthetics.

Fields, Annie. *Life and Letters of Harriet Beecher Stowe.*
    Boston and New York: Houghton Mifflin Co., 1898.
    Fields was a personal friend of HBS. Fields emphasizes
    Stowe's sense of spiritual mission to bring reform.
    The book is composed mainly of Stowe's letters.

Foster, Charles H. *The Rungless Ladder*. Durham, North
    Carolina: Duke University Press, 1954.   HBS reacts to
    the death of two unregenerate sons, until her "inner
    compulsions" were resolved in Episcopalianism.   However,
    she gives a "final yes" to Calvinism in *The Minister's
    Wooing* when Hopkins gives up his claims to Mary in
    "disinterested benevolence."   The issue of Stowe's
    degree of Calvinism is a major controversy among HBS
    scholars.

Gilbertson, Catharine. *Harriet Beecher Stowe*. New York:
    Kennikat Press, 1937.   HBS' "outlet for unsatisfied emo-
    tion and distress" was religion as seen in the religious
    themes of her novels.

Johnston, Johanna. *Runaway to Heaven*. New York: Doubleday
    & Co., 1963.   HBS rebelled from bondage "of the spirit,"
    that is, from Calvinism "based on death, torment, and
    wrath."   She was also sometimes motivated by "fearful
    fascination with the dark aspects of lust."   It was as
    a writer that she could run away from what was unpleas-
    ant in her life.   Seems to rely on Gilbertson.

McCray, Florine T. *The Life-Work of the Author of Uncle
    Tom's Cabin*. New York: Funk and Wagnalls, 1889.   An
    unauthorized biography, by an author who was acquainted
    with HBS.   Gives background for her novels in her reli-
    gious views, namely her modification of harsh theology.

Rourke, Constance. *Trumpets of Jubilee*. New York: Harcourt,
    Brace, and Co., 1927.   HBS attacked Lyman, Calvin Stowe,
    and Calvinism and their dominion over her.   She felt
    downtrodden like black slaves.   She defeated "the old
    enemy Calvinism" in Hopkins in *The Minister's Wooing*.
    She identified with her woman-child heroines who are
    powerful (Nina, Mary, Mara, Dolly, and Lady Byron as
    well).   She replaced Calvinism with morality and with
    death without horror.

Stowe, Charles Edward. *Harriet Beecher Stowe: The Story of
    Her Life*. Boston and New York: Houghton Mifflin Co.,
    1911.   Written with HBS' approval, it is mainly composed
    of her letters, many of which are published in other
    books as well.   He maintains that HBS attended the
    Episcopal Church in order to be with her daughters.
    Some valuable letters on spiritualism and the afterlife.

Stowe, Charles and Lyman Stowe. *Harriet Beecher Stowe: The
    Story of Her Life*. Boston and New York: Houghton
    Mifflin Co., 1911.   HBS was greatly influenced in her
    theology of love by theologians Catharine and Edward.

Harriet and Henry were not theologians but preachers.
All the Beechers shared the sense of mission. Samuel
Hopkins in *The Minister's Wooing* is her attempt to show
that "even the stern hereditary faith of New England
had in its elements of tenderness and beauty."

Stowe, Lyman. *Saints, Sinners, and Beechers*. Indianapolis:
     Bobbs Merrill Co., 1934. Roxana and Catharine drew
     Lyman away from strict Calvinism. The Beecher children
     saw themselves as God's agents responsible for reform
     in the world; "to do right was their religion rather
     than to believe right." In her novels Harriet preached
     that God was love.

Wagenknecht, Edward. *Harriet Beecher Stowe: The Known and
     the Unknown*. New York: Oxford University Press, 1965.
     HBS rejected "barbarous theology."

Wilson, Edmund. *Patriotic Gore*. New York: Oxford Univer-
     sity Press, 1962. Blacks are HBS' religious spokesper-
     sons in her anti-Calvinism. She exposed the "pernicious
     effects of Calvinism," motivated by her own suffering.
     No other writer has "produced, in the form of fiction,
     such a chronicle of religious history" spanning the end
     of the eighteenth century to the 1870s.

Wilson, Forrest. *Crusader in Crinoline*. Philadelphia,
     London: J. B. Lippincott, 1941. HBS provided "the coup
     de grace" to the old Calvinist dogmas and "their cruel
     consistencies." She "marked the beginning of a more
     liberal and emotional type of religious observance."
     Harriet was repressed by her older brothers and sisters,
     and was the family's spiritual problem-child, but they
     also believed that she was a genius.

THEOLOGICAL AND RELIGIOUS INFLUENCES

Addison, James T. *The Episcopal Church in the United States*.
     Hamden, Conn.: Archon Books, 1969.

Ahlstrom, Sidney E. *A Religious History of the American
     People*. New Haven: Yale University Press, 1972.

Ahlstrom, Sidney E., ed., *Theology in America: The Major
     Protestant Voices*. New York, Indianapolis: Bobbs-
     Merrill Co., 1967.

Ayres, Anne. *The Life and Work of William Augustus Muhlenberg*.
     New York: Harper & Brothers, 1880.

Baxter, Richard. *The Saints' Everlasting Rest*. London: Thomas Kelly, 1836.

Beecher, Lyman. *The Reform of Society: Four Sermons, 1804-1828*. New York: Arno Press, 1972.

Bellamy, Joseph. *True Religion Delineated*. Worcester, Mass.: American Antiquarian Society, "Early American Imprint Microcard Collection," Microcard 6462; reprint ed., Boston: Kneeland, 1750.

Billington, Ray A. *The Protestant Crusade, 1800-1860*. New York: MacMillan Co., 1938.

Bushnell, Horace. *Women's Suffrage: The Reform Against Nature*. New York: Scribner & Sons, 1869.

Butler, Joseph. *The Analogy of Religion*. New York: Frederick Ungar Publishing Co., 1961; first published 1736.

Chorley, E. Clowes. *New Movements in the American Episcopal Church*. New York: Charles Scribner's Sons, 1946.

Clebsch, William A. *American Religious Thought--A History*. Chicago: University of Chicago Press, 1973.

Cross, Barbara M., ed. *Autobiography of Lyman Beecher*. 2 Vols. Cambridge, Mass.: Belknap Press, 1961.

Daly, Mary. *Beyond God the Father: Toward a Philosophy of Women's Liberation*. Boston: Beacon Press, 1973.

DeMille, George E. *The Catholic Movement in the American Episcopal Church*. Philadelphia: Church Historical Society, 1941.

Dodds, Elisabeth. *Marriage to a Difficult Man: the "Uncommon Union" of Jonathan and Sarah Edwards*. Philadelphia: Westminister Press, 1971.

Elkins, Hervey. *Fifteen Years in the Senior Order of Shakers*. Hanover, New Jersey: Dartmouth Press, 1853.

Foster, Frank Hugh. *A Genetic History of the New England Theology*. New York: Russell and Russell, Inc., 1963.

Gabriel, Ralph Henry. *Religion and Learning at Yale: The Church of Christ in the College and University, 1757-1957*. New Haven: Yale University Press, 1958.

Gaustad, Edwin. *The Great Awakening in New England.* New
York: Harper, 1957.

Gilman, Charlotte Perkins. *His Religion and Hers: A Study
of Our Fathers and the Work of Our Mothers.* New York
and London: The Century Co., 1923.

Greene, M. Louise. *The Development of Religious Liberty in
Connecticut.* Freeport, New York: Books for Libraries
Press, 1970; originally published 1905.

Haroutunian, Joseph. *Piety Versus Moralism: The Passing of
the New England Theology.* Hamden, Conn.: Archon Books,
1964.

Heimert, Alan and Perry Miller. *The Great Awakening.* New
York: Bobbs-Merrill Co., 1967.

Heimert, Alan. *Religion and the American Mind.* Cambridge,
Mass.: Harvard University Press, 1966.

Henry, Stuart C. *Unvanquished Puritan: A Portrait of Lyman
Beecher.* Grand Rapids, Mich.: William B. Erdmans, 1973.

Hill, Samuel, et al. *Religion and the Solid South.* Nashville: Abington Press, 1972.

Hudson, Winthrop S. *American Protestantism.* Chicago: The
University of Chicago Press, 1961.

    Religion in America. New York: Scribner, 1965, revised
ed., 1974.

Hutchison, William. *The Transcendentalist Ministers.* Boston:
Beacon Press, 1965.

Ide, Jacob, ed. 3 Vols. *The Works of Nathaniel Emmons, DD.*
Boston: Crocker and Brewster, 1842.

Johnson, Charles A. *The Frontier Camp Meeting.* Dallas:
Southern Methodist University Press, 1955.

Keller, Charles. *The Second Great Awakening in Connecticut.*
Hamden, Conn.: Archon Books, 1968.

Littell, Franklin H. *The Church and the Body Politic.* New
York: Seabury Press, 1969.

Loetscher, Lefferts A. *A Brief History of the Presbyterians.*
Philadelphia: The Westminister Press, 1958.

McLoughlin, William G., ed. *The American Evangelicals,*
1800-1900, An Anthology. New York: Harper and Row,
1968.

The Meaning of Henry Ward Beecher: An Essay on the
Shifting Values of Mid-Victorian America, 1840-1870.
New York: Alfred A. Knopf, 1970.

Modern Revivalism: Charles Finney to Billy Graham.
New York: Ronald Press Co., 1959.

New England Dissent, 1630-1833. 3 Vols. Cambridge,
Mass.: Harvard University Press, 1971.

Manross, William W. *A History of the American Episcopal*
Church. New York: Morehouse-Gorham Co., 1959.

Marsden, George. *The Evangelical Mind and the New School*
Presbyterian Experience: A Case Study of Thought and
Theology in Nineteenth Century America. New Haven and
London: Yale University Press, 1970.

Mead, Sidney. *The Lively Experiment: The Shaping of Chris-*
tianity in America. New York: Harper & Row, 1963.

Nathaniel William Taylor, 1786-1858, A Connecticut
Liberal. Hamden, Conn.: Archon Books, 1967.

Meyer, Donald. *The Positive Thinkers.* New York: Doubleday,
1965.

Miller, Perry. *Errand Into the Wilderness.* Cambridge:
Harvard University Press, 1956.

Jonathan Edwards. New York: World Publishing Co., 1963.

The Life of the Mind in America: From the Revolution
to the Civil War. New York: Harcourt, Brace and World,
1965.

Nature's Nation. Cambridge, Mass.: Belknap Press, 1967.

ed. *The American Transcendentalists.* New York: Doubleday Anchor Books, 1957.

Miller, Perry and Thomas Johnson. *The Puritans.* 2 Vols.
New York: Harper Torchbooks, 1963.

Munger, Theodore L. *Horace Bushnell.* Boston: Houghton
Mifflin Co., 1899.

New, John F. H. *Anglican and Puritan: The Basis of Their Opposition, 1558-1640.* Stanford, California: Stanford University Press, 1964.

Nicholes, James Hastings. *Romanticism in American Theology: Nevin and Schaft at Mercersburg.* Chicago: University of Chicago Press, 1961.

O'Dea, Thomas. *The Mormons.* Chicago: University of Chicago Press, 1957.

Piercy, Josephine. *Anne Bradstreet.* New York: Twayne, 1965.

Powell, Milton. *The Voluntary Church in America.* New York: MacMillan, 1967.

Russell, Letty M. *Human Liberation in a Feminist Perspective-- A Theology.* Philadelphia: Westminster Press, 1974.

Schneider, Herbert W. *A History of American Philosophy.* New York: Columbia University Press, 1948.

Smith, Chard Powers. *Yankees and God.* New York: Hermitage House, 1954.

Smith, James and A. Leland Jamison, eds. *Religion in American Life.* 2 Vols. Princeton, New Jersey: Princeton University Press, 1961.

Smith, John E., ed. *Works of Jonathan Edwards, Vol. 2, Religious Affections.* New Haven, Conn.: Yale Univ. Press, 1959.

Sweet, William W. *The American Churches.* London: Epworth Press, 1947.

Religion in the Development of American Culture, 1765- 1840. Gloucester, Mass.: P. Smith, 1963.

Religion on the American Frontier; Vol. 2, The Presbyterians. New York: Harper & Brothers, 1930.

Trinterud, Leonard. *The Forming of an American Tradition.* Philadelphia: Westminister Press, MCMXLIV.

Tuveson, Ernest. *Redeemer Nation: The Idea of America's Millenial Role.* Chicago: Univ. of Chicago Press, 1968.

Walzer, Michael. *The Revolution of the Saints.* Cambridge, Mass.: Harvard University Press, 1965.

Weiseberger, Bernard. *They Gathered at the River: The Story of the Great Revivalists and Their Impact Upon Religion in America*. Chicago: Quandrangle Books, 1966.

Whalen, William J. *Minority Religions in America*. New York: Society of St. Paul, 1972.

Winslow, Ola Elizabeth. *Jonathan Edwards, 1703-1758: A Biography*. New York: MacMillan Co., 1940.

Wright, Conrad. *The Beginnings of Unitarianism in America*. Boston: Starr King Press (distributed by Beacon Press), 1955.

INTELLECTUAL HISTORY

Abel, Darrel. *The Literature of the Atlantic Culture*. New York: Barron's Educational Series, 1963.

Adams, Henry. *The Education of Henry Adams*. New York: Modern Library, 1931.

Barzun, Jacques. *Classic, Romantic and Modern*. New York: Anchor Books, Doubleday & Co., 1961.

Basch, Francoise. *Relative Creatures: Victorian Women in Society and the Novel*. New York: Schocken, 1970.

Beaty, Frederick L. *Light from Heaven: Love in British Romantic Literature*. Dekalp, Ill.: Northern Illinois University Press, 1971.

Beecher, Catharine and Harriet Stowe. *The American Women's Home*. New York: J. B. Ford, 1870.

Bernbaum, Ernest. *Guide Through the Romantic Movement*. New York: Ronald Press Co., 1949.

Best, Mary Agnes. *Rebel Saints*. New York: Harcourt, Brace & Co., 1925.

Blackwell, Antoinette. *The Sexes Throughout Nature*. New York: Putnam and Sons, 1875.

Borchard, Ruth. *John Stuart Mill: The Man*. London: C. A. Walts, 1957.

Brown, Herbert Ross. *The Sentimental Novel in America, 1789-1860*. Durham, North Carolina: Duke Univ. Press, 1940.

Bushnell, Horace. *Woman's Suffrage: The Reform Against
    Nature*. New York: C. Scribner & Co., 1869.

Byron, Lord. *The Complete Poetical Works of Lord Byron*.
    Durham, North Carolina: Duke University Press, 1940.

    The Complete Works of Lord Byron. New York: MacMillan
    Co., 1906.

Carter, Paul A. *The Spiritual Crisis of the Gilded Age*.
    DeKalb, Ill.: Northern Illinois Univ. Press, 1971.

Eddy, Mary Baker. *No and Yes*. Boston: First Church of
    Christ, Scientist, 1891.

    Retrospection and Introspection. Boston: First Church
    of Christ, Scientist, 1918.

    Science and Health. Boston: First Church of Christ,
    Scientist, 1875.

Erikson, Erik. "Inner and Outer Space: Reflecting on
    Womanhood," in Robert Lifton, ed., *The Woman in America*.
    Boston: Beacon Press, 1964.

Farnham, Eliza. *Woman and Her Era*. 2 Vols. New York:
    A. J. Davis & Co., 1864.

Fiedler, Leslie A. *Love and Death in the American Novel*.
    New York: Criterion Books, 1970.

Fuller, Arthur, ed. *Woman in the Nineteenth Century and
    Kindred Papers*. New York: The Tribune Association, 1869.

Fuller, Margaret. *Woman in the Nineteenth Century*. Boston:
    Roberts Brothers, 1895.

Gilson, Mrs. Claude. *Unpublished Biography of Antoinette
    Blackwell*. Schlesinger Archives, Radcliffe College.

Gohdes, Clarence, ed. *Essays on American Literature in Honor
    of Jay B. Hubbell*. Durham, North Carolina: Duke Univ.
    Press, 1967.

Grimké, Sarah. *Letters on the Equality of the Sexes*. New
    York: Burt Franklin, 1910.

Harveson, Mae Elizabeth. *Catharine Esther Beecher: Pioneer
    Educator*. Phil.: The Science Press Printing Co., 1932.

Himmelfarb, Gertrude. *Victorian Minds*. New York: Alfred
    A. Knopf, 1968.

Hofstadter, Richard. *Social Darwinism in American Thought*.
    Boston: Beacon Press, 1955.

Houghton, Walter. *The Victorian Frame of Mind*. New Haven:
    Yale University Press, 1957.

Kelley, Robert. *The Transatlantic Persuasion*. New York:
    Alfred Knopf, 1969.

Kiely, Robert. *The Romantic Novel in England*. Cambridge,
    Mass.: Harvard University Press, 1972.

Lewis, G. *Impressions of America and the American Churches*.
    New York: Negro Universities Press, 1964.

Lewis, R. W. B. *The American Adam: Innocence, Tragedy and
    Tradition in the Nineteenth Century*. Chicago: Univ.
    of Chicago Press, 1955.

McPhersen, Aimee Semple. *In the Service of the King: The
    Story of My Life*. New York: Boni & Liverwright, 1927.

May, Henry. Introduction to HBS, *Old Town Folks*. Cambridge,
    Mass.: Belknap Press of Harvard Univ. Press, 1966.

Mill, John S. *Dissertations and Discussions*. London:
    Parker, M. D. CCCLIX.

    The Subjection of Women. London: Longmans, Green, 1869.

Milmine, Georgine. *The Life of Mary Baker Eddy and the His-
    tory of Christian Science*. New York: Doubleday, Page
    & Co., 1909.

Morgan, Edmund. *The Puritan Family*. New York: Harper &
    Row, 1966.

Mosse, George. *The Culture of Western Europe*. New York:
    Rand McNally Co., 1961.

Neumann, Erich. *The Great Mother: An Analysis of the
    Archetype*. New York: Pantheon Books, 1963.

Parrington, Vernon Louis. *The Romantic Revolution in
    America*. New York: Harcourt, Brace and Co., 1927.

Pattee, Fred Lewis. *The Feminine Fifties*. New York:
    D. Appleton-Century Co., 1940.

Piercy, Josephine. *Anne Bradstreet*. New York: Twayne
    Publishing Co., 1965.

Roszak, Betty and Theodore Roszak. *Masculine/Feminine.* New
    York: Harper & Row, Harper Colophon Books, 1969.

Scott, Sir Walter. *Ivanhoe.* 2 Vols. Boston: Estes &
    Lauriat, 1893.

Sklar, Kathryn. *Catharine Beecher: A Study in American
    Domesticity.* New Haven: Yale University Press, 1973.

Stanton, Elizabeth Cady, et al. 2 Vols. *The Woman's Bible.*
    New York: European Publishing Co., 1895.

Taylor, William R. *Cavalier and Yankee.* London: W. H.
    Allen, 1963.

Thistlewaite, Frank. *America and the Atlantic Community:
    Anglo-American Aspects, 1790-1850.* New York: Harper
    and Row, 1959.

Titus, Francis. *Narrative of Sojourner Truth.* New York:
    Arno Press, 1968; first published Battle Creek, Mich.,
    1878.

Tocqueville, Alexis de. *Democracy in America.* 2 Vols. New
    York: Schocken, 1961.

Veblen, Thorsten. *The Theory of the Leisure Class.* London:
    MacMillan Co., 1899.

Wade, Mason. *Margaret Fuller: Whetstone of Genius.* New
    York: Viking Press, 1940.

Wharton, Edith. *The Age of Innocence.* New York: New Ameri-
    can Library, 1943.

White, Elizabeth Wade. *Anne Bradstreet: The Tenth Muse.*
    New York: Oxford University Press, 1971.

Wright, Henry. *The Empire of the Mother.* Boston: William
    White, 1870.

SOCIAL HISTORY

Anderson, Charles H. *White Protestant Americans.* Englewood
    Cliffs, New Jersey: Prentice Hall, 1970.

Banner, James M. *To the Hartford Convention: The Federal-
    ists and the Origins of Party Politics in Massachusetts,
    1789-1815.* New York: Knopf, 1970.

Barber, John W. *Historical Collections, Massachusetts.*
Worcester: Dorr, Howland Co., 1839.

Beecher, Catharine E. *An Essay on Slavery and Abolitionism
With Reference to the Duty of American Females.* Freedom, New York: Books for Libraries Press, 1970; first
published in 1837.

   *The Evils Suffered by American Women and American
   Children.* New York: Harper & Brothers, 1846.

Benson, Lee. *The Concept of Jacksonian Democracy.* Princeton, New Jersey: Princeton University Press, 1961.

Billington, Ray A. *The Protestant Crusade.* New York:
MacMillan Co., 1938.

Butler, Charles. *The American Lady.* Philadelphia: Hogan
and Thompson, 1830.

Carroll, E. Malcolm. *Origins of the Whig Party.* Gloucester,
Mass.: Peter Smith, 1964.

Charnwood, Lord, and R. Godfrey. *Abraham Lincoln.* New York:
Henry Holt & Co., 1917.

Clappe, Louise. *The Shirley Letters.* Santa Barbara, Calif.:
Peregrine, 1970.

Cole, Charles C. Jr. *The Social Ideas of the Northern Evangelist, 1826-1860.* New York: Columbia University
Press, 1954.

Cross, Barbara. *Educated Women in America.* New York:
Teachers' College Press, 1965.

Cross, Whitney R. *The Burned-Over District.* Ithaca:
Cornell University Press, 1950.

Donald, David. *Charles Sumner and the Coming of the Civil
War.* New York: Knopf, 1961.

Dunbar, Janet. *The Early Victorian Women.* London: Harrop,
1953.

Elkins, Hervey. *Fifteen Years in the Senior Order of Shakers.*
Hanover, New Jersey: Dartmouth Press, 1853.

Federal Writers Project, WPA. *Connecticut.* Boston: Houghton Mifflin Co., 1938.

Federal Writers Project, WPA. *Florida*. New York: Oxford
     University Press, 1939.

Federal Writers Project, WPA. *Maine, A Guide "Down East"*.
     Boston: Houghton Mifflin Co., 1937.

Filler, Louis. *The Crusade Against Slavery*. New York:
     Harper & Row, 1960.

Firestone, Shulamith. *The Dialectic of Sex: The Case for
     Feminist Revolution*. New York: Bantam Books, 1970.

Fischer, David H. *The Revolution of American Conservatism*.
     New York: Harper & Row, 1965.

Flexner, Eleanor. *Century of Struggle*. New York: Atheneum,
     1972.

Foner, Eric. *Free Soil, Free Labor, Free Men*. New York:
     Oxford University Press, 1970.

Formisano, Ronald P. *The Birth of Mass Political Parties,
     Michigan, 1827-1861*. Princeton, New Jersey: Princeton
     University Press, 1971.

Frederickson, George M. *The Black Image in the White Mind*.
     New York: Harper & Brothers, 1971.

Friedan, Betty. *The Feminine Mystique*. New York: Dell
     Publishing Co., 1963.

Friedman, Jean and John Shade, eds. *Our American Sisters:
     Women in American Life and Thought*. Boston: Allyn and
     Bacon, 1973.

Furnas, J. C. *Goodbye to Uncle Tom*. New York: William Sloan
     Associates, 1956.

Gornick, Vivian and Barbara Moran, eds. *Women in Sexist
     Society*. New York: Signet Books, 1971.

Green, Constance M. *American Cities in the Growth of the
     Nation*. Welwyn, Garden City, Great Britain: John
     de Graff, 1957.

Handlin, Oscar. *Immigration as a Factor in American History*.
     Englewood Cliffs, New Jersey: Prentice-Hall, 1959.

          Race and Nationality in American Life. Boston: Little,
     Brown & Co., 1957.

Higham, John. *Strangers in the Land*. New Brunswick, New
    Jersey: Rutgers University Press, 1955.

Hogeland, Ronald W., ed. *Women and Womanhood in America*.
    Lexington, Mass.: D. C. Heath, 1973.

Howe, Daniel W. *The American Whigs*. New York: John Wiley
    & Sons, 1973.

Koenig, Samuel. *Immigrant Settlements in Connecticut*.
    Hartford, Conn.: Connecticut State Department of Edu-
    cation, 1938.

Kraditor, Aileen. *The Ideas of the Woman Suffrage Movement,
    1890-1920*. New York: Doubleday, 1971.

    Means and Ends of American Abolitionism. New York:
    Pantheon Books, 1969.

Lee, W. Storrs. *The Yankees of Connecticut*. New York:
    Henry Holt Co., 1957.

Lifton, Robert Jay, ed. *The Woman in America*. Boston:
    Beacon Press, 1967.

Litchfield County, Connecticut. Philadelphia: J. W. Lewis
    & Co., 1881.

Livermore, Shaw, Jr. *The Twilight of Federalism*. Princeton,
    New Jersey: Princeton University Press, 1962.

Marden, Charles and Gladys Meyer. *Minorities in American
    Society*. New York: American Book Co., 1968.

Morse, Anson E. *The Federalist Party in Massachusetts to
    the Year 1800*. Princeton, New Jersey: Princeton Univ.
    Library, 1909.

Myers, Gustauvs. *History of Bigotry in the United States*.
    New York: Random House, 1943.

Nevins, Allan. *The Emergence of Lincoln*. New York: Charles
    Scribners' Sons, 1950.

Nordhoff, Charles. *The Communistic Societies in the United
    States*. New York: Hillary House Publishers, 1960.

O'Neill, William. *Everyone Was Brave: The Rise and Fall of
    American Feminism*. New York: Doubleday, 1969.

    The Women's Movement: Feminism in the United States.
    New York: Barnes and Noble, 1969.

Ormsby, Robert M. *A History of the Whig Party.* Boston:
     Crosby, Nichols & Co., 1859.

Papashvily, Helen. *All the Happy Endings: A Study of the
     Domestic Novel in America.* New York: Harper, 1956.

Parker, Gail. *The Oven Birds.* New York: Doubleday, 1972.

Peters, Samuel. *A General History of Connecticut.* Freeport,
     New York: Books for Libraries Press, 1969; first pub-
     lished in 1877.

Quincy, Josiah. *Municipal History of the Town and City of
     Boston During Two Centuries (1630-1830).* Boston:
     Charles C. Little & James Brown, 1832.

Rabb, Theodore and Robert Rotberg, eds. *The Family in
     History.* New York: Harper and Row, 1971.

Rawley, James A. *Race and Politics.* New York: J. P.
     Lippincott, 1969.

Riegel, Robert. *American Women: A Story of Social Change.*
     Rutherford, New Jersey: Fairleigh Dickinson University
     Press, 1971.

Robinson, Marie. *The Power of Sexual Surrender.* New York:
     Signet, New American Library, 1959.

Roszak, Betty and Theodore Roszak. *Masculine/Feminine:
     Readings in Sexual Mythology and the Liberation of
     Women.* New York: Harper Colophon Books, 1969.

Rust, Richard, ed. *Glory and Pathos: The Response of Nine-
     teenth Century Americans to the Civil War.* Boston:
     Holbrook Press, 1970.

Ryan, Mary P. "American Society and the Cult of Domesticity,
     1830-1860," UCSB Ph.D. Dissertation, August, 1971.

Schnir, Miriam. *Feminism: The Essential Historical Writings.*
     New York: Random House, 1972.

Sillens, Samuel A. *Women Against Slavery.* New York: Masses
     and Mainstream, 1955.

Smith, Page. *Daughters of the Promised Land.* Boston:
     Little, Brown, 1970.

Smith, Timothy. *Revivalism and Social Reform.* New York:
     Abingdon Press, 1957.

Trollope, Frances. *Domestic Manners of the Americans*. New
    York: Knopf, 1949.

Tyler, Alice Felt. *Freedom's Ferment*. New York: Harper &
    Row, 1932.

Walker, Alexander. *Woman Physiologically Considered*. New
    York: Langly, 1843.

Wilson, Edmund. *Patriotic Gore*. New York: Oxford Univer-
    sity Press, 1962.

Vicines, Martha, ed. *Suffer and Be Still: Women in the
    Victorian Age*. Bloomington: Indiana University Press,
    1973.

APPENDIX 1

HARRIET BEECHER STOWE - A CHRONOLOGY

1811   Born Litchfield, Connecticut, June 14.

1816   Mother, Roxana, died.

1822   Catharine's fiancé, Alexander Fisher, died.

1824   Moved to Hartford to be a pupil and later teacher in Catharine's school.

1829   Full-time teacher.

1832   Moved to Cincinnati.

1836   Married Calvin Stowe, Biblical scholar. Seven children, all but the last born in Cincinnati.

1843   *The Mayflower* published (short stories about New England).

1847   Son Charles died in epidemic.

1850   Moved to Bowdoin College in Brunswick, Maine. Last child born.

1852   *Uncle Tom's Cabin*. Moved to Andover, Massachusetts.

1853   *A Key to Uncle Tom's Cabin* published.

1854   Aided in research for Lyman's autobiography, *Sunny Memories of Foreign Lands*.

1853, 56, 59 - Toured Europe.

1856   *Dred*

1857   Son Henry drowned.

1859   *The Minister's Wooing*

1862   *The Pearl of Orr's Island*

1862   *Agnes of Sorrento*

1863   Father, Lyman, died. and Calvin retired.

1864   Moved to Hartford. *Household Papers*.

204 The Religious Ideas of Harriet Beecher Stowe:
Her Gospel of Womanhood

1867	*Religious Poems*
1868	*Men of Our Times, The Chimney Corner*
1869	*Old Town Folks*
1868-84	Winters spent in Mandrin, Florida.
1870	Son Frederick disappeared in San Francisco. *Lady Byron Vindicated*
1871	*Old Town Fireside Stories, Pink and White Tyranny, My Wife and I*
1873	*Palmetto Leaves*
1875	*We and Our Neighbors*
1877	*Footsteps of the Master*
1878	*Bible Heroines, Poganuc People*
1896	Died Hartford, Connecticut.

APPENDIX 2

A CHRONOLOGY OF HBS' INVOLVEMENT WITH THE

ANTI-SLAVERY CRUSADE

1833   First viewed slaves at work for a few hours during a visit to a Kentucky plantation.

1835   Theodore Weld led a revolt against the Lane trustees which resulted in a migration of the majority of students and faculty to Oberlin to carry out their abolitionist policies.

1836   George Beecher was converted to abolitionism by Weld. Cincinnati race riots; a mob damaged the abolitionist press of James G. Birney (*The Philanthropist*); Henry Ward Beecher armed himself to confront the mob. Wilson believed that Henry and Harriet became secret abolitionists as a result.

1837   HBS wrote, "There needs to be an intermediate society. If not...all the excesses of the abolition party will not prevent humane and conscientious men from joining it." (C. E. Stowe, *Life of HBS*, p. 37).

1839   A black woman servant of the Stowes' was sought for her former owner; Henry Beecher and Calvin Stowe spirited her away at night to hide her with friends in the country. (HBS later said the underground railroad ran through their house.)

1841   Cincinnati race riots lasted for four weeks. *The Philanthropist* office was sacked. The military had to take over the town. Charles Beecher worked as a clerk in New Orleans and provided accounts of plantation life. (One of his stories provided the basis for Simon Legree.)

1850   HBS wrote her first public protest against the Fugitive Slave Law.

1851   HBS wrote "The Two Altars," her first anti-slavery fiction. She began *Uncle Tom's Cabin*, serialized in the *National Era* from June 8, 1851 to April 1, 1852. She corresponded with Garrison, Frederick Douglas, and acted as a go-between for the two abolitionists. Douglas and Sojourner Truth visited her in Andover.

1853   *The Key to Uncle Tom's Cabin* was published.
       She visited England and was greeted as a heroine for
       her authorship of *Uncle Tom's Cabin*.

1854   In response to the Kansas-Nebraska act she wrote "An
       Appeal to the Women of America" (to circulate peti-
       tions, hire lecturers, circulate copies of speeches,
       and above all, to pray) published in the *Independent*.
       She corresponded with Sumner and other statesmen. She
       organized a petition which was signed by 3,050 clergy-
       men and presented to the Senate in protest against
       slavery.

1856   *Dred* was serialized in the *Independent*. She supported
       Fremont's presidential candidacy.

1859   She decided to cease anti-slavery work because she
       predicted "a crisis" which nobody could greatly help
       or hinder." (Wagenknecht, *Harriet Beecher Stowe*,
       p. 246.)

1859   She praised John Brown's raid on Harper's Ferry.

1860   She took no part in the election campaign.

1861   By September 6, she called for immediate emancipation,
       was disgruntled with Lincoln.
       She attacked Lincoln's First Inaugural Address.

1862   In November her "Address to Women in England" was pub-
       lished in the *Atlantic Monthly*. She visited Lincoln
       before she wrote the address.

1863   In January's issue of the *Atlantic Monthly* she rebuked
       Britain for her support of the Confederacy.
       The Emancipation Proclamation was signed; she received
       an ovation in the New York Music Hall, and felt her
       mission was achieved.

1865   She supported Johnson's conciliatory Reconstruction
       policy. She came out against Negro suffrage because
       she thought it could not work in the South. She
       supported desegregated schools.

STUDIES IN WOMEN AND RELIGION

Gayle Kimball is associate professor of women's studies at California State University at Chico. She also edited **Women's Culture: The Women's Renaissance of the Seventies** (Scarecrow), and wrote **The So/So Marriage** (Beacon).